Moderate Drinking[SM]

My Way

A Woman's All-Natural Program
to Control Alcohol and Get the Most Out of Life!

Donna J. Cornett, M.A.
Drink/Link Moderate Drinking Programs

People Friendly Books

Moderate Drinking My Way^{SM}

A Woman's All-Natural Program to Control Alcohol
and Get the Most Out of Life!

People Friendly Books

For Information Address:
People Friendly Books
P.O. Box 5441
Santa Rosa, CA 95402 USA
www.drinklinkmoderation.com

ISBN 0-9763720-8-8

Library of Congress Control Number: 2011919512

Printed in the United States of America 2012

To my Parents, Shirley and Lester Cornett -
I am a reflection of you.

To my Auntie Rene -
Sweet and strong. You will always be a part of me.

Contents

Introduction

I'm a former problem drinker with a background in psychology and I've counseled thousands of drinkers since 1985. Probably seventy percent of my clients have been women. And after years of looking at the big picture of women and alcohol, it's clear to me that women drink for different reasons than men, they have different drinking styles and patterns than men, they seek treatment for different reasons than men and they respond to different treatment approaches compared to men.

That's why I wrote *Moderate Drinking My Way* - the first female-friendly, drug-free moderate drinking program for any woman who wants a take it or leave it attitude about alcohol. It empowers you to drink less, improve your drinking habits, prevent alcoholism and dig deeper to resolve women-specific issues that drive you to drink. But it's more than just an alcohol program, it's a lifestyle program that promotes a moderate drinking mindset and way of life - eliminating your desire to drink naturally so you not only reduce your alcohol consumption, you live your life to the fullest!

Adapted from the Drink/Link Moderate Drinking Program which I developed in 1988, this approach offers women a drinking and life-style makeover. A change from the inside out. It encourages them to fix their problems and themselves in healthy ways - instead of worrying and waiting for things to get better with a cocktail in their hand. And when women are offered a kinder, gentler female-oriented alcohol abuse prevention program that inspires them to take a more active role in their lives, they'll drink less.

In general, men drink to demonstrate their masculinity, independence and stamina. They drink to feel more powerful and to bond with other men. But women drink for different reasons. Liquor is often used to suppress or express unacceptable feelings and as a form of self-treatment for depression, stress or loss. Essentially, women drink to soothe their inner world - because they don't think they can manage their outer one.

Men's and women's drinking styles and patterns also vary. Men openly party at bars, sporting events, on the golf course or in front of the TV. It's no secret. Women, on the other hand, tend to veil their drinking. They dream up events and excuses to imbibe - game nights, play dates, book clubs or nights out with the girls. They may drink before their partner gets home from work or after the kids are in bed. And some go underground and hide their drinking.

For the most part, men think differently about alcohol and drinking problems too. Their black and white thinking assumes that if you have an issue with booze, you must be an alcoholic. And the only alternatives to treat any type of alcohol abuse are to stop drinking and go to AA. But women see these areas in shades of gray. Many believe that having a drinking problem doesn't necessarily make you an alcoholic. And compromising with a moderate drinking approach is a practical solution for them.

The women I've spoken to also seem more motivated to tackle heavy drinking early on, instead of waiting until they're hooked, compared to men. Women I've talked to are more concerned about the effects of alcohol on their health, relationships and parenting than men. And they have an intense personal desire to do something about dangerous drinking before it destroys them and their family. In fact, the most powerful motivating factors for many women to control their drinking are their needs to maintain their family and be a good wife, mother and role model for their kids. Many men, on the other hand, address their drinking only after they've been forced to. External factors and coercion - their spouse threatening to leave them or their employer threatening to fire them if they don't stop drinking - get men into treatment.

Why we've lumped men's and women's alcohol abuse treatment together for so long is a mystery to me. One size does not fit all. And, unfortunately for women, most alcoholism, recovery and treatment programs, including AA, are based on men's experiences and don't work all that well for women. So offering men and women the same treatment approaches and goals, even though the reasons behind their drinking and for them getting help are miles apart, simply doesn't make sense.

Another reason why I wrote this book stems from my own bout with problem drinking. Years ago when I was drinking too much my only options at the time were to continue to drink or to quit and attend AA meetings. But I knew I wasn't that far gone - I didn't have any alcohol-related problems and lifelong abstinence seemed like overkill to me. That's why I developed the Drink/Link Moderate Drinking Program in the first place. Lifelong abstinence seems like overkill to lots of other women drinkers too. So they put off doing anything about their drinking problem and become alcoholic. Offering women a female-friendly early intervention just seemed liked the next logical step to me.

My sister's drinking also sparked my interest in putting together a moderate drinking program specifically for women. Dale, my sister, was an alcoholic for years before she died of cirrhosis of the liver and pancreatitis at the age of fifty-five. She never tried to change or quit and we all lived with the consequences of her drinking for years. Why did she take refuge in vodka? Why didn't she ever try to cut down or stop? Her drinking tore my family apart and I wonder what her life would have been like if she'd had access to a treatment program designed just for women.

Alcohol abuse among women is a growing health and social problem too. Liquor is their drug of choice and the number of women who drink has sharply increased. Sixty percent of American women drink, six million of them abuse alcohol or are dependent on it and twenty-five percent of alcoholics in this country are women. Women from the ages of twenty-one to thirty-four suffer the highest rates of problem drinking and thirteen percent of all women drinkers engage in heavy binge drinking.

And girls are starting to experiment with booze at a younger age and they're catching up and downing just as much as boys these days. Approximately one-third of all girls have had their first drink before high school. In fact, the average age for a girl to have her first drink is less than thirteen years old! Nearly half of all high school girls drink and more than one in four is a binge drinker - drinking five or more drinks on the same occasion at least once in the last thirty days. Unfortunately, the earlier a girl starts drinking, the more likely she'll have trouble with liquor later in life. Alcohol abuse among females is on the rise and a fresh, new approach might help them head off a more serious problem down the road.

Women also metabolize spirits differently than men. They get drunk faster, become addicted more easily and develop alcohol-related diseases earlier than men. More ethanol gets into a woman's bloodstream and directly into her system - including her heart, brain and liver - and does more damage to her body, compared to men. Just another important reason to get women into treatment earlier.

And women are less likely to get help specifically for alcohol abuse. They seek treatment from their doctor or psychologist or psychiatrist for fatigue or depression instead. Often, these professionals don't screen for alcohol problems, so many women's drinking is never diagnosed or treated. And they continue to hit the bottle. If we offered women a kinder moderate drinking intervention, more might admit to a drinking problem, get help and avoid years of alcohol abuse.

There's also a double standard for women when it comes to drinking. Women are more stigmatized by alcohol abuse than men. Drinking women are stereotyped as loud, unladylike, loose, sexually aggressive and adulterous. Not exactly the feminine ideal. A drunk woman is disgusting because she's considered a slut and a whore and has abandoned her traditional roles of wife and mother. But these same stereotypes and attitudes don't apply to hard drinking men.

Women who drink recklessly have more relationship problems - especially with partners and children. Their husbands leave them more often and they're more likely to get divorced and have child custody problems than women who don't have issues with alcohol. Drinking women are also more likely to become victims of domestic violence and be verbally, physically and emotionally abused. They're more inclined to have unsafe sex too.

Heavy drinking women are twenty-five times more likely to feel like failures in their roles of wife, mother and nurturer than women who don't drink problematically. They feel more ashamed and embarrassed about their drinking than men and see themselves as inadequate when it gets out of hand. Their self-esteem is shot because of their alcohol use and it's hard to recover once it's been damaged. Consequently, they may down even more booze to ease their psychological pain.

Alcoholic women are more likely to use several drugs and develop a cross-addiction to over-the-counter or prescriptions drugs. Their careers often suffer because their work quality and productivity are poor. They have more accidents and women who drink are five times more likely to commit suicide compared to women who don't have problems drinking. Excessive drinking can negatively impact every aspect of a woman's life - physically, psychologically, spiritually, interpersonally, professionally, financially and legally.

There are a few moderate drinking options for women out there. But they oversimplify the subject, don't address the distinct issues behind women's drinking and push pharmaceutical drugs as a means to cut down and change drinking behavior. And, most important, they don't work long-term. Improving drinking habits and attitudes is a lot more complex than popping a pill! And pharmaceutical solutions to problem drinking proposed by people writing under pseudonyms for drug companies won't prevent alcohol abuse.

Moderate Drinking My Way is a revolutionary breakthrough for women and women's healthcare and fills a huge void in the alcohol abuse treatment field. It's a gentler alternative that will get females into treatment earlier - reducing alcoholism rates for women everywhere!

It's for any woman who drinks and wants a take it or leave it attitude about alcohol. It's for any woman who is concerned about her drinking. It's for any woman who wants to make liquor less important in her life. It's for any woman who has a history of alcohol abuse in her family and doesn't want to become an alcoholic. It's for any woman who's in a relationship affected by booze. It's for any drinking woman who's raising kids and wants to be a good role model for them. It's for any woman who wants to lead a healthy, happy, fulfilling life free from alcohol abuse.

Hopefully, mothers will hand *Moderate Drinking My Way* down to their daughters, sisters will give it to their sisters, aunts will offer it to their nieces, friends will lend it to their friends, doctors will prescribe it to their patients and alcohol abuse treatment professionals will dispense it to their clients.

We can defeat the growing alcohol abuse epidemic among women worldwide with *Moderate Drinking My Way*!

Cheers,
Donna Cornett
Founder and Director
Drink/Link Moderation Programs and Products
Moderate Drinking My Way Program

Disclaimer

Moderate Drinking My Way is not recommended for the alcoholic, anyone who has a serious drinking problem, anyone who has a physical or psychological condition caused or aggravated by alcohol use, anyone who suffers from serious health, psychological, social, legal, financial or work-related problems as a result of alcohol use, any woman who is pregnant or thinking of becoming pregnant or anyone who has successfully abstained. This book does not advocate or encourage anyone who is under the legal drinking age of twenty-one to drink alcohol. Results vary according to the individual.

My Story:

How I Developed a Drinking Problem and Beat It!

I hit bottom in my mid-thirties. Not from alcohol. No, I hit bottom psychologically, socially, financially and spiritually. And I felt lonely, angry, frustrated, unfulfilled, underrated, depressed and powerless. Where was my knight in shining armor I'd been waiting for? Coming to rescue me? Wasn't I supposed to be married by now? Having a family? Working at something I loved? Earning enough money to support myself comfortably? Having healthy relationships with good friends who treated me well? Wasn't my family supposed to be there for me through thick and thin?

Unfortunately, none of the wonderful people and events I had expected to enjoy at this time in my life had materialized. I was miserable and thought there was something terribly wrong with me. I felt like a failure - with no way out. It was me against the world and the only time I wasn't hurting or unhappy was when I was staring at the bottom of an empty wine glass. All of my pain, rage, frustration, depression, loneliness and worthlessness began to melt away after one drink. After two drinks, life looked even better. And by the third, I finally was happy. I was drinking my problems and feelings away and my destructive drinking pattern was beginning to develop.

The feeling I was becoming dependent on alcohol was also developing. And that scared me and put me back to square one. Now, I was not only trying to drink my troubles away, but the concerns I had about my drinking too. If I continued to drink heavily, I thought, I could even become an alcoholic. Just what I needed. Another problem making me even more miserable!

The Seeds of My Problem Drinking Are Sown

What had gone so terribly wrong that I started to rely on booze to make my life bearable? Let's start from the beginning. I was a normal kid growing up in a normally dysfunctional middle class family. My family consisted of me, my three sisters and my parents. We had lots of relatives - a big catholic family full of cousins, aunts and uncles. We went to catholic school. We had our issues, but no one became a serial killer.

Women in my family - including me - were expected to be passive, conforming and supportive. Men were in charge and you followed their lead because they made the living and knew best - no matter what. And if you didn't get with the program, you were taught to simply stuff your feelings. Put up or shut up.

This passive female role requiring you to obey your man at all cost never really worked for me. It implied women were second-class citizens and their sole purpose in life was to serve men. Women looked like victims to me too. Always sacrificing themselves to take care of others. And I hated the idea of being a victim. Needless to say, I felt stifled by the women's roles and expectations I was born into and I'm sure those feelings and rebelling against them sowed the first seeds of my drinking problem.

I certainly wasn't pressured by my parents to be or do anything special. They never pushed me to go to school or have a career. In fact, I was the one who insisted on going to college and getting a degree. My mom and dad just assumed I'd get married out of high school and have a family. All of the women in my family were stay-at-home moms and seemed content in the traditional roles of wife and mother. And if I wasn't going to marry young, then I'd probably go to beauty school or work at the post office. But the thought of me being a housewife, beautician or postal worker for the rest of my life drove me crazy. No, I had bigger ideas. I was going to graduate from college - the first person in my family to do so. I wanted to be more and do more than the women before me. And my ambitious attitude probably sowed even more problem drinking seeds.

I was one of the middle children. You know, the middle kids who have to make a lot of noise so they can be heard - because mom and dad are so busy tending to the baby and praising the oldest child they never pay much attention to you. My little sister Dale, the baby, was the center of attention and got anything she wanted. Which was a curse for her in the end. She had a serious drinking problem, but instead of practicing a little tough love and not putting up with her alcohol-fueled antics, the family indulged her in every way - except for me and a few other family members. Codependency and enabling were alive and well in the Cornett household and from the age of twenty-two on, Dale drank so much vodka every day she died from alcoholism at the age of fifty-five. She ultimately wasted away from pancreatitis and cirrhosis of the liver - not an easy way to go.

Volumes have been written about alcoholic family dynamics and ours was textbook. Our family revolved around Dale's alcoholism. Dale - because of her drinking and all of her alcohol-related problems - was the focus of our family for forty years and anyone who challenged her was in hot water. Her dishonesty, brushes with the law and trips to the emergency room were to be overlooked and swept under the rug. And anyone who didn't enable her was put down and ostracized from the family. We were taught you stand by your family through thick and thin. And alcoholism was no exception. So if I criticized Dale or offered a more enlightened approach to deal with her so she'd stop drinking, I was dismissed as an unloving, unsupportive kook. I was the bad guy and black sheep of the family for years because of this issue. But I could not in good conscience support the alcoholic family system that kept Dale drinking.

In our family the "normal" kids - my sisters and I who didn't have problems with drugs or alcohol - went unnoticed. Our good graces and achievements weren't acknowledged because the alcoholic kid, Dale, was the needy one and was always the in the spotlight. And I resented it. I was always put on the back burner in favor of my rabble-rousing alcoholic sister. And more problem drinking seeds were sown in my young adult life.

My family did not have a history of alcohol abuse. When I was growing up, liquor was reserved for only very special occasions. In fact, drinking only happened three or four times a year when I was a kid - maybe on a holiday or at a party. But when my father got into a new, more upscale line of business where you were expected to have a cocktail after work, the vodka tonic at five became a daily ritual for everyone. Everything stopped when it was happy hour - in favor of drinking. It was a time to bond with other family members - in spite of our differences. Fortunately, this family drinking pattern hadn't formed until I was away at college.

In college, I was spoiled with interesting friends and had the time of my life. Foot-loose and fancy-free, I explored the world in more ways than one and had a ball. Even though I had a great social life and a moneyed boyfriend, I was a serious student. I didn't want bad grades to jeopardize my good time. And booze and drugs played a minor role in my college years. I was high on life and didn't need any substance to have fun.

I came crashing down after college though. After earning a master's degree in psychology, it was time for me to either settle into a job or continue on in school. But I was tired of school and the thought of me working at a starting position in psychology bored me to tears. I wanted to party and I did - supporting myself with meaningless, dead-end jobs that just paid the bills. And the wonderful people and friendships I had made in college and thought I could depend on forever began to fade. I gradually lost touch with old friends and started hanging out with people I'd met at work who didn't have much on the ball. These relationships were ones of convenience. I really didn't have a lot in common with these people except work and play.

I also had an uncanny ability to pick bad men. Good-looking, superficial types who weren't interested in anything serious. They were out for what they could get - with no strings attached. Sometimes, I was even the object of their verbal, emotional and physical abuse. Why did I pick these jerks? Maybe because in the beginning of the relationship they gave me what I wanted. An attractive mate to keep me company. Maybe I picked them because my self-esteem was so low I didn't think I could do any better. I certainly didn't feel good about myself or my life so how could I expect to have a healthy relationship with a normal guy. I was heartbroken often. And problem drinking seeds were really taking root.

After ten years on this bittersweet treadmill of my young adult life - running with the wrong crowd, being used and abused by bad men, estranged from my family, working dead-end jobs to make ends meet - I felt more lonely, depressed, worthless and powerless than ever. I was drinking more than ever too. Three to four glasses of wine every night was my cure-all for my feelings and predicament. And problem drinking was becoming just one more thing for me to worry about.

Problem Drinking in Full Bloom

Even at the height of my despair and heavy drinking I wasn't an alcoholic. I didn't have any health, social, work, legal or financial problems because of my drinking. In fact, I was quite health conscious. I exercised regularly, went out of my way to eat right and got plenty of rest. Everything you're supposed to do to take good care of yourself. My health and looks were important to me so I tried to maintain myself, even though I was hitting the bottle.

I rarely got drunk or had a hangover. I never had a blackout. I never binged or went on a bender. I never got into fights, had a DUI or a health problem because of my drinking. I never missed important meetings, appointments or work because of my drinking. Booze never kept me from fulfilling important obligations. I never obsessed about that first cocktail, but I did look forward to it. And none of my friends or my doctor ever told me to cut down because they were concerned about my drinking. In fact, most of my pals at the time drank more than I did!

But those three or four glasses of wine every night bothered me. I knew it wasn't normal and I was worried about where I'd be in ten years if I let it slide. Surely, I'd be an alcoholic by then, I thought. I'd be in the gutter. How much longer could my poor body hold up - after being bombarded with booze every night? I'd get sick in five or ten years, maybe even die from alcoholism. But I kept on drinking anyway. At a loss about what to do.

I really had a love/hate relationship with liquor. On the one hand, I loved my wine. That cocktail was the highlight of my day. It was my mood enhancer. It was my stress reducer. It was my entertainment. It was my best friend. It was my party for one. It was my quick fix for everything. Having a bad day? Have a drink. Feeling financially strapped? Have a drink. Fighting with the boyfriend? Have a drink. Problems at work? Have a drink. Lonely? Have a drink. Frustrated? Have a drink. Angry? Have a drink. Depressed? Have a drink. It was my magic elixir to escape or cope with problems and feelings. But on the other hand, I was disgusted with myself for leaning on a substance to get by. Wine was becoming too important to me. I was depending on it more and more to be happy. It was becoming a habit. I was getting hooked on it and I hated that feeling. I was torn. And I lived with this peculiar love/hate relationship for some time.

The only other substance I had ever felt an unhealthy need for was nicotine. Years before, I had smoked cigarettes. My habit grew from a couple of cigarettes a day to four packs in a few short years. I was so addicted to tobacco that if I ran out of smokes before I went to bed at night, I'd have to run to the store and pick some up to make sure I had my morning puffs. When I realized how dependent I was on tobacco, I was horrified I was so controlled by a substance. I knew I had a monkey on my back. But there was no cutting down with cigarettes. Stopping cold turkey was my only option because I intuitively knew I could not control my smoking. I had to stop altogether and that's what I did. I truly understood the nature of addiction after my bout with nicotine and I didn't want to go down that same road with liquor too. I knew I wasn't addicted to wine yet, so if there was anything I could do - short of stopping - I'd do it.

Thinking back, I was the classic problem drinking female. And I knew I wasn't alone. I'd seen many other women go down the same path. A path strewn with identity and role resentment and confusion, complicated family relationships, toxic romantic relationships, non-existent self-esteem and feelings of depression and powerlessness. Is it any wonder why I liked liquor so much? Wine was the most convenient, socially acceptable and fastest acting fix to lift my spirits, fill the void and deal with life. But it was the easy way out and I didn't want to become an alcoholic!

I wanted to stop this runaway train, but I didn't know how. At the time, the only options in the United States for problem drinkers like me were to stop drinking and go to AA. And I did attend a couple of AA meetings. I found them interesting and right up my alley in a way - with my background in psychology I was all for baring one's soul to change for the better. But I couldn't relate to the gruesome war stories I'd heard. And I didn't have any alcohol-related problems yet. I wasn't that far gone. Besides, I had trouble with the concept of a higher power. I thought abstinence and AA were fine for some people, but not for me.

I wasn't addicted to wine yet and I didn't want to be. I wanted to do something about my drinking before it was too late and I was out of control, but what?

Goodbye Problem Drinking, Hello Moderate Drinking!

How did I turn my drinking and my life around? I kept my eyes and ears open and began my "alcohol education" - learning more about alcohol, drinkers and treatment. I learned about the disease concept of alcoholism which really doesn't have any scientific evidence to support it. I learned that in the United States anyone with a "drinking problem" was considered to be "alcoholic", which is not necessarily true. I learned that most people thought "problem drinking" and "alcoholism" were the same thing, even though they're not. I learned that problem drinkers outnumber alcoholics four to one in this country. I learned that alcoholism usually doesn't happen overnight and it takes years for most drinkers to graduate to it. And I learned that if you can catch a drinking problem early on, you're still capable of returning to responsible, problem-free drinking.

Then, on my way back from connecting with just another bad boyfriend who lived in Europe, I had a chance meeting in England with the director of DrinkWatchers. Now defunct, DrinkWatchers was a program that taught drinkers how to manage alcohol and drink less. It wasn't for alcoholics and it wasn't an abstinence program. Eureka! This might be the answer I'd been looking for to beat my own drinking problem, I thought. I'd try this program and if it worked for me, it might work for other American drinkers too. Drinkers who were just like me - not alcoholics or people who were experiencing serious alcohol-related problems - but problem drinkers who wanted to exercise some control over their alcohol use and reduce their consumption.

When I got home I did more research into moderate drinking programs. And I discovered they not only existed in the United Kingdom, but in Sweden, Australia and New Zealand as well. They were a well-guarded secret and taboo in the United States though. AA and the alcohol treatment professionals in this country believed if a moderate drinking program was made available, alcoholics would use it as an excuse to continue to drink and it would put the traditional treatment industry out of business.

These early moderate drinking approaches worked for a lot people. They offered very basic guidelines - like setting drink limits and using simple behavioral tools to pace drinking. And these basics did help me to cut down. But I soon realized these simple guidelines were only the beginning. So I added more behavioral, cognitive, motivational and lifestyle strategies and techniques and developed the Drink/Link Moderate Drinking Program in 1988.

By this time I had also tackled many of the underlying issues in my life that had driven me to drink in the first place. I resolved them in healthy ways - which reflected positively on my drinking and my life. I was taking better care of myself, I was doing something meaningful with my life and I was associating with people who respected me and treated me well - which increased my self-esteem and self-confidence. So between these lifestyle changes and practicing the strategies and skills I offered in Drink/Link, I was drinking less naturally and was happier in general.

Within a few short years, my drinking was no longer an issue and light, guilt-free drinking had become second nature to me. Alcohol was less important to me and I had acquired a moderate drinking mentality. In fact, my sensible drinking behavior, attitudes and lifestyle all supported and complemented one another - which has resulted in my long-term success. Heavy drinking was no longer a monkey on my back and I now enjoyed a take it or leave it attitude about wine.

As a result of my personal experiences with drinking, I became passionate about preventing alcohol abuse worldwide. And I've devoted my life to offering problem drinkers commonsense solutions to clean up their drinking habits and reduce their alcohol consumption.

The Moderate Drinking My Way Program Sprouts

The Moderate Drinking My Way Program is specifically for women and is an offshoot of the Drink/Link Moderate Drinking Program. After so many years of treating women suffering from alcohol abuse, I thought it was high time we had our own female-friendly approach to prevent problem drinking.

This program not only shows you how to cultivate a take it or leave attitude about alcohol, drink less and improve your drinking behavior, it also encourages you to dig deeper and address the problems that drive you to drink in healthy ways. It's more than just a moderate drinking program, it's a lifestyle program that promotes wholesome thinking and living - eliminating your desire to drink naturally and empowering you to live your life to the fullest!

The Moderate Drinking My Way Program involves five steps. In the first one, you learn about drinking and alcohol. In the second step, you explore your particular drinking styles and patterns. Next, you jumpstart your healthy new drinking habits with simple guidelines and clinically-proven tips. Fourth, you fix the underlying issues that trigger your drinking and work on a moderate drinking mindset and lifestyle. And finally, you discover how to maintain your sensible new drinking habits and attitudes forever.

You're going to tackle your drinking on several different levels too. You're going to learn how to motivate yourself to stick the program even when the going gets tough. You're going to use the moderate drinking tools and concepts in the program to help you stay within your drink limits. And you're going to reward yourself when you succeed at staying on track. All important components of behavior change.

Take your time when completing the program and book. Devote at least one week to each chapter so you can fully digest all of the information in it before you move on to the next. And practice everything you learn at least two times. That way you'll know what works for you and what you should continue to practice. Answer all of the questions and complete all of the exercises too. You'll gain insight into your drinking and yourself if you do. Also, read the chapters in order. Don't skip around. You'll get the most out of the program that way.

By the end of the book you should be drinking less, enjoying a take it or leave it attitude about alcohol and getting the most out of life - without prescription drugs. You will have corrected the issues that have caused your drinking and you'll no longer be wasting your precious energy worrying about problem drinking and it's effects on you. In fact, if you apply everything you learn in the program to your drinking and your life, you're guaranteed reduced alcohol consumption! Safe drinking will come effortlessly to you and you'll never struggle with an unhealthy desire to drink again!

You don't have to hit bottom! I'm living proof you can change your drinking behavior and your life for the better. Just get with the program!

Start Thinking About Your Story . . .

I was the typical problem drinking woman. Leaning on liquor to escape and cope with feelings and circumstances I thought were beyond my control. Alcohol use and abuse escalating over the years because of role and identity issues, low self-esteem, toxic relationships and feelings of depression and despair.

My story may be your story. Or maybe you can relate to only a few of the feelings and situations that I dealt with. Or maybe your story is completely different - involving an entirely unique set of circumstances and emotions. Everyone has their own story - when, where, why and how their dangerous drinking developed. And the sooner you become aware of yours, the sooner you'll be able to put your bad habits behind you and replace them with healthy new ones.

Before long, you'll examine the reasons that drive many women to drink. Then, when you're crystal clear about the factors in your life that have led to your drinking problem, you'll be asked to write your story. The more aware you are of these alcohol-triggering issues, the less you'll drink!

Step One

Get Smart About Your Drinking and Alcohol

Chapter 1

How Does Liquor Affect You and Your Life?

J ust knowing the impact that alcohol has on you and your life will help you to get a handle on it. So the smarter you are about the physical, health, psychological, interpersonal, social, spiritual, professional, financial and legal effects of booze, the easier it will be for you to cut down!

How Do You Metabolize Alcohol?

Women are more sensitive to spirits than men. We have a higher proportion of body fat which contains less water, compared to men, so alcohol is more concentrated in our bodily fluids. One factor that makes us more susceptible to it than men.

Women also have less of an enzyme in their stomach lining that metabolizes liquor, compared to men. Consequently, more alcohol enters into our bloodstream and liver and we get higher on the same amount than a man. We become physically and mentally impaired faster than men and this effect is intensified if we diet or don't eat. We stay high longer than a man too.

Women's hormonal levels can slow the rate of alcohol metabolism in their body. And oral contraceptives can slow our alcohol metabolism rate too. A couple more reasons why we become more compromised than men when we drink.

And a woman's tolerance to booze declines with age. We process it less efficiently and it stays in our bloodstream longer the older we get. Just another factor that makes us more sensitive to spirits.

How Does Alcohol Affect Your Body and Brain?

Your Blood Alcohol Concentration (BAC) measures the amount of alcohol in your bloodstream. The higher your BAC is, the higher you are. Refer to the Blood Alcohol Concentration Charts for both men and women below.

How loose do you get on one, two and three drinks over one, two and three hours? Take note, then compare your BACs to the BACs for men of the same weight having the same number of drinks over the same time periods. See the difference? Women register higher BACs than men.

Next, look at the How Does Alcohol Affect You Chart - describing the physical and psychological changes you experience at different BACs. Notice when you're under a .06 BAC, you're relaxed and have a sense of well-being. You're also becoming mentally and physically impaired. But when you hit a higher BAC - higher than a .06 - that's when things get dicey. You become less inhibited, your reasoning fails and your physiological functions and reflexes go down hill fast. And it just gets worse. When you reach a .08 BAC, you've lost it and you're legally drunk. You're loud, emotional, staggering, slurring your words and your motor control and reaction times are shot. You're a mess.

The next time you drink, stop and assess the physical and psychological changes happening inside of your body and brain after every drink. Wouldn't it be great if you could determine your BAC just by keeping track of your feelings and sensations?

Blood Alcohol Concentration Charts

Women's BAC Chart

Drinks	100	120	140	160	180	200	220	240	
0	.00	.00	.00	.00	.00	.00	.00	.00	Only Safe Driving Limit
1	.05	.04	.03	.03	.03	.02	.02	.02	
2	.09	.08	.07	.06	.05	.05	.04	.04	Driving Skills Impaired
3	.14	.11	.10	.09	.08	.07	.06	.06	
4	.18	.15	.13	.11	.10	.09	.08	.08	
5	.23	.19	.16	.14	.13	.11	.10	.09	
6	.27	.23	.19	.17	.15	.14	.12	.11	Legally Intoxicated
7	.32	.27	.23	.20	.18	.16	.14	.13	
8	.36	.30	.26	.23	.20	.18	.17	.15	
9	.41	.34	.29	.26	.23	.20	.19	.17	
10	.45	.38	.32	.28	.25	.23	.21	.19	Possible Death

1 drink equals roughly 1.5 ounces of 80 proof hard alcohol or 1 ounce of 100 proof hard alcohol, 1 12oz. beer, or 1 5oz. glass of wine.

Men's BAC Chart

Drinks	100	120	140	160	180	200	220	240	
0	.00	.00	.00	.00	.00	.00	.00	.00	Only Safe Driving Limit
1	.04	.03	.03	.02	.02	.02	.02	.02	
2	.08	.06	.05	.05	.04	.04	.03	.03	Driving Skills Impaired
3	.11	.09	.08	.07	.06	.06	.05	.05	
4	.15	.12	.11	.09	.08	.08	.07	.06	
5	.19	.16	.13	.12	.11	.09	.09	.08	
6	.23	.19	.16	.14	.13	.11	.10	.09	
7	.26	.22	.19	.16	.15	.13	.12	.11	Legally Intoxicated
8	.30	.25	.21	.19	.17	.15	.14	.13	
9	.34	.28	.24	.21	.19	.17	.15	.14	
10	.38	.31	.27	.23	.21	.19	.17	.16	Possible Death

1 drink equals roughly 1.5 ounces of 80 proof hard alcohol or 1 ounce of 100 proof hard alcohol, 1 12oz. beer, or 1 5oz. glass of wine.

How Does Alcohol Affect You Chart

Blood Alcohol Concentration	Changes in Feelings and Personality	Physical and Mental Impairments
0.01 – 0.06	Relaxation Release of Well-being Loss of Inhibition Lowered Alertness Joyous	Thought Judgment Coordination Concentration
0.06 – 0.10	Blunted Feelings Disinhibiting Extroversion Impaired Sexual Pleasure	Reflexes Impaired Reasoning Depth Perception Distance Acuity Peripheral Vision Glare Recovery
0.11 – 0.20	Over-Expression Emotional Swings Angry or Sad Boisterous	Reaction Time Gross Motor Control Staggering Slurred Speech
0.21 – 0.29	Stupor Lose Understanding Impaired Sensations	Severe Motor Impairment Loss of Consciousness Memory Blackout
0.30 – 0.39	Severe Depression Unconsciousness Death Possible	Bladder Function Breathing Heart Rate
⇨ 0.40	Unconsciousness Death	Breathing Heart Rate

How Does Alcohol Affect Your Health?

Liquor can be a blessing or a curse for a woman. It depends on how you use it. Short-term, you get loaded faster and stay drunk longer than a man. And you blackout sooner if you drink heavily. FYI, a blackout occurs when you drink too much too fast and you can't remember the drinking party the next day. Heavy alcohol use may also interfere with your sleep - interrupting your REM sleep stage and causing you to wake frequently. So after a night of hard drinking, you're not only hung over, you're also sleep deprived.

Long-term, here's the bad news. Unfortunately, there's plenty of it. Women are more vulnerable to alcohol-related health problems which we develop sooner than men. And even though fewer women drink than men, among the heaviest drinkers, women equal or surpass men in the number of health problems that result from alcohol use. Female alcoholics also have higher death rates than those of male alcoholics, including deaths from stroke, heart disease, cirrhosis of the liver, suicides and alcohol-related accidents.

If you're a big drinker, you're at greater risk of developing cirrhosis of the liver and other liver diseases sooner and at lower levels of drinking than a man. And if you diet or don't eat when you drink, you increase your chances of liver damage. When you drink, about five percent of the booze in your bloodstream is excreted through your lungs, sweat, saliva and urine and the rest is removed by your liver. No wonder your liver is one of the first organs to go if you're a heavy drinker. When you abuse alcohol, fatty deposits build up in your liver and this fat accumulates, crowds out and eventually kills your healthy liver cells. Your liver becomes tender, swollen and inflamed - a condition known as alcoholic hepatitis. If you stop or cut down on your drinking, eat well and take care of yourself, this condition can be reversed. But if you continue to hit the bottle, scar tissue forms in the organ which leads to cirrhosis of the liver which can be fatal.

Your pancreas can also take a beating if you're a problem drinker. Too much liquor can lead to pancreatitis, a dangerous condition where the pancreas becomes inflamed. It causes severe pain in the upper abdomen, lower chest and back and nausea, vomiting and constipation. And it can be life threatening. You're also more likely to develop digestive and nutritional problems, such as gastritis, malnutrition, anemia,

25

peptic ulcers, intestinal bleeding and a folic acid deficiency which causes severe diarrhea.

Heart disease is the number one killer of women and spirits can be a contributing factor to it. Women at any age who drink in excess are at increased risk for cardiovascular diseases, such as coronary artery disease, arrhythmias and cardiomyopathy. One study found that women who drank six or more drinks per day were eight times more likely to develop cardiomyopathy, a degenerative disease of the heart muscle. And chances are you'll develop high blood pressure on just two or three drinks a day!

Your endocrine system can be injured by alcohol - causing menstrual irregularities, infertility and early menopause. And if you're pregnant and abusing alcohol, you could have a spontaneous abortion or your child could be born with fetal alcohol syndrome.

You might also increase your risk of breast cancer. Some research strongly suggests the more you drink, the greater your chances of developing breast cancer because booze raises estrogen levels. But other studies have found the same incidence of breast cancer for all women. More research is needed to determine the exact relationship between breast cancer and alcohol.

And excessive drinking can cause osteoporosis. Too much liquor causes you to excrete calcium at twice the normal rate - which will lead to osteoporosis. Another downside to imbibing too much, too often.

Hard drinking suppresses your immune system - making you more susceptible to infections and pneumonia. In fact, you become more vulnerable to disease in general.

Booze affects the brains of alcohol abusers too. It impairs your learning ability, memory, abstract thinking, problem-solving and perceptual motor skills. And women are more likely to suffer from alcohol-induced brain damage than men. Women who drink too much have smaller brains in early middle age after fewer years of heavy drinking than alcohol-abusing men.

You not only increase your risk of health problems if you overdrink, you also become more accident prone. Older women who have more than one drink a day have more falls and other accidents. Drinking women are also at increased risk of suicide. Women who drink are five times more likely to commit suicide compared to women who don't drink. Too much alcohol could lead to your demise one way or another - from illness, accidents or suicide.

But there is some good news if you keep your drinking in check. Long-term, the Harvard Nurses Study found women who were light to moderate drinkers lived longer than non-drinkers or heavy drinkers. And moderate alcohol consumption may actually decrease your risk of heart attacks as you get older. As you age your estrogen levels drop, but a little alcohol raises them - reducing the likelihood of blood clots and increasing your good HDL cholesterol - which might prevent heart disease. Light drinking may also prevent osteoporosis. Again, it raises your estrogen levels which help you to retain and metabolize calcium. The best news is, however, if you stick to sensible drinking you'll avoid all of the awful problems associated with alcohol abuse!

Keep the pros of moderate drinking and the cons of heavy drinking in mind throughout the program. They might motivate you to lighten up!

How Has Alcohol Complicated Your Life?

If you started young and engaged in adolescent binge drinking, you might have encountered some pretty dangerous situations that changed the course of your life forever. You not only increased your chances of dying from alcohol poisoning, you also increased your odds of having unprotected sex, getting pregnant or being the victim of a sexual assault. Teenage girls who are big drinkers are five times more likely to have sex and one third less likely to use protection than girls who don't drink.

If you were a reckless drinker as a teenager, you probably didn't excel in school either. And poor academic performance when you were young may have had a huge negative impact on your life as an adult. Maybe you didn't make it into college because you didn't have the grades. If you did get into college, maybe you flunked out because of too much partying. Maybe menial, meaningless jobs were the only ones you could get because of your lack of education. And you might have had legal problems - DUI's, arrests for public drunkenness, vandalism or assault when you were under the influence.

Excessive drinking may be taking a toll on your relationships regardless of your age. Family, friends and employers may be concerned about you because you behave irresponsibly and don't fulfill important obligations, like getting to work on time, paying your bills or taking care of your kids, when you're drinking excessively. When you're looped, you may lose control and become so uninhibited you say or do things you'd never dream of saying or doing if you weren't loaded. You may have mood swings when you imbibe or get mean - alienating your partner, kids, family and friends.

You're more likely to get a divorce if you drink too much. Men tend to divorce alcohol-abusing wives while women tend to stick with alcohol-abusing husbands. You're also more likely to be the victim of domestic abuse and violence if you're a hard drinker. And you're more inclined to have unsafe sex and sexual problems if you hit the bottle. FYI, women in treatment for alcoholism report high rates of sexual problems, including lack of desire and difficulty achieving orgasm.

Odds are you'll have child custody battles too. If you drink problematically, your ex could bring this to the attention of the court when it's deciding child custody matters. And courts do not like to place innocent children with mothers who abuse alcohol. They think you're irresponsible and may endanger or neglect your children.

Your job or career may also be on the line because of your fondness for drink. You're hung over often - which makes it difficult for you to concentrate at work. In addition to being slow, indecisive and forgetful, the quality of your work and your productivity suffer. And you're often late and take lots of sick days because of too much fun the night before.

If you're demoted or fired because of your drinking, you'll certainly have money problems. But even if you're working and earning a paycheck but you're blowing it all on booze, you could be stretched financially. Spending a significant portion of your income on liquor in restaurants, bars, clubs or at home is a serious sign of alcohol abuse.

Brushes with the law can also point to problems with spirits. Driving drunk is the most obvious. Getting nabbed once is an expensive and inconvenient lesson, but if you're arrested more than once for drunk driving you may serve jail time and/or have your license revoked or restricted, not to mention forking over thousands for fines, court fees and lawyers to settle the matter. Taking a cab is so much safer and cheaper than driving drunk! Fighting, domestic abuse and irresponsible behavior in general when you're high could also land you in the slammer.

Finally, the psychological toll you may be paying for destructive drinking might be the last straw. Hating yourself and thinking you're a lousy wife, mother and person because you drink too much is so shameful. And your reputation - what your partner, kids, family, friends, employer and community think of you - may also be taking a hit. When your precious self-esteem and reputation are in tatters because of too much booze, it's hard to recover them.

So many serious health, psychological, relationship, social, spiritual, school, money legal and work problems can be caused by alcohol abuse. Which ones can you relate to?

Do You Have a Drinking Problem?

Honestly answer the questions below to see where you stand with alcohol:

- Have you ever felt bad or guilty about your drinking?
- Have you ever wanted to cut down on your drinking?
- Have you ever had health problems because of your drinking?
- Has your doctor ever advised you to cut down or stop drinking?
- Have your family, friends or employer ever expressed concern to you about your drinking?
- Have you ever had an argument with your family, friends or employer about your drinking?
- Do you get drunk often?
- Do you have hangovers often?
- Do you think your alcohol consumption has gone up over the last year?
- Do you drink longer than you intend to?
- Have you ever had a blackout? Where you forget what you said or did when you were drinking the night before?
- Have you ever missed an important appointment, failed to look after your kids or called in sick to work because you were drinking or recovering from a hangover?
- Have you ever been fired or demoted from a job because of your drinking?

- Have you ever had a DUI or any other legal problems because of your drinking?
- Does it take more and more alcohol for you to get high?
- Are you unable to stop drinking once you've started?
- Have you ever had a drink in the morning to steady your nerves or to nurse a hangover?
- Do you obsess about that first drink of the day?
- Do you hide your drinking or drink in secret at times?

If you answered yes to any one of these questions, you've got a drinking problem and the sooner you acknowledge it, the better. Address it now - instead of drinking your life away - and go on to lead a healthy, happy life!

∞ Chapter 2 ∞

Why Do Women Drink?

Y our desire to drink and your drinking are the result of a complex interaction of many direct and indirect factors, including biological and psychological tendencies, family influences, relationship issues and life experiences to name just a few.

On the one hand, women drink for the same reasons as men - to relax and have fun. And drinking is triggered by obvious internal or external cues, like people, places, situations, emotions or moods.

On the other hand, there are deeper female-specific issues that can trigger women's drinking, like conflict over one's identity or role as a woman, sexual, physical or emotional abuse, complicated relationships, low self-esteem, psychological states and life transitions. And we tend to use liquor to escape or cope with these issues, instead of trying to resolve them in healthy ways. Unfortunately, that's when harmful drinking happens.

Now you're going to explore both the obvious and underlying factors in your life that might have started you drinking and are keeping you drinking. Then, a little later in the program, you're going to discover how to handle each and every one of these concerns so they no longer result in heavy drinking.

Obvious Drinking Cues That Trigger Both Men's and Women's Drinking

Hunger, thirst, pain or fatigue can be internal drinking cues for both men and women. You drink because you're hungry, you drink because

31

you're thirsty, you drink because you hurt or you drink because you're tired. Liquor satisfies your hunger, quenches your thirst, relieves your pain or energizes you.

Feelings and moods can also trip your need to drink. You drink to enhance a good mood. Or to lift yourself up if you're down. Or to take the edge off of loneliness or boredom. Common internal drinking cues for many people.

Drinking places, companions and circumstances are external cues that can cause excessive drinking too. If you guzzle at certain places - at home, a friend's house, at a restaurant, club or pub - these places are drinking cues for you. If you overdo it when you're with your partner or a friend, these individuals are drinking cues for you. Situations or circumstances, like parties, play dates, girl's night out, weddings, holidays, game night or sporting events, may also lead to heavy drinking for you. Or perhaps the mere sight, sound or smell of booze can stimulate your alcohol appetite.

What internal and external drinking cues start you thinking about drinking and can cause you to overdrink? Physiological sensations? Emotions? Moods? People? Places? Circumstances? The sights and sounds of spirits? List them.

Underlying Issues That Trigger Women's Drinking Specifically

Genetic and Biological Factors

You may have a genetic predisposition for problem drinking. Look at your family history of alcohol use and abuse. If one or both of your parents is an alcoholic, if one or more of your siblings is an alcoholic or if you have several family members who are alcoholics, you may have inherited a genetic predisposition for alcohol abuse and you're at greater risk for alcoholism. It's important to note, however, that no one gene or set of genes has actually been found to cause alcoholism. Instead, there may be certain genes that predispose you to it. And you don't have to be born with a genetic predisposition for alcoholism to become an alcoholic. In fact, fifty to sixty percent of people who become alcoholics have no family history of it.

If you're the child of an alcoholic, you're four to ten times more likely to become an alcoholic, compared to a child who has no close relatives who are alcoholics. You're also more likely to start drinking at a younger age and develop a drinking problem early on. And people with a family history of alcoholism are less likely to outgrow a drinking problem, compared to people with no family history of it.

Girls whose mothers drank moderately or heavily during pregnancy are six times more likely to drink alcohol than girls whose mothers did not drink during pregnancy. There is strong evidence of a relationship between prenatal exposure to alcohol and drinking among girls even when taking into account other factors, like current maternal drinking, child-rearing practices and problem behaviors in childhood. But no relationship has been found between maternal drinking during pregnancy and alcohol use among boys.

If you have a genetic predisposition for dangerous drinking, you might have a higher tolerance for liquor so you need more of it to get high. Or you may be more sensitive to the positive effects of it than the average drinker - like feeling more relaxed and comfortable in social settings - so you keep on chugging when others stop.

It's also possible your alcohol problem resulted from too much drinking when you were young and your brain wasn't yet fully developed. Your brain continues to grow and mature into your twenties and this long developmental period may account for impulsive, thrill-seeking behavior. During this time you're into new experiences, including experimenting with drugs and alcohol. So if you pushed the limits with beer and drank too much when you were young, it may have caused brain damage leading to alcoholism later in life.

Does alcohol abuse or alcoholism run in your family? Do you think your tolerance to alcohol is higher than most drinkers? Do you think you're more sensitive to the positive effects of alcohol and enjoy drinking more than most drinkers? Did you drink heavily when you were young - before your brain was fully developed - and do you think this has affected your drinking today?

Personality Characteristics

You may have certain personality characteristics that have influenced your drinking. You may be very impulsive - you have spontaneous, sudden thoughts and engage in erratic behavior without thinking of the consequences of your actions - which might be behind your reckless drinking.

Or you may be overly interested in new experiences and thrill-seeking adventures. Experimenting with drugs and alcohol and seeing how much and how fast you can drink can lead to destructive drinking.

Hyperactivity can also trigger drinking problems. When you're excited or manic, you might use spirits to calm yourself down or to regulate your mood.

Girls with Childhood Conduct Disorder are almost five times more likely than those without a history of the disorder to develop alcoholism. Childhood Conduct Disorder symptoms include being verbally and physically aggressive towards others, anti-social behavior involving a disregard for rules or laws, destruction of property or animal cruelty and a lack of empathy or remorse. Girls with this disorder may be rejected by their peers and be attracted to risk-taking individuals who drink in excess.

Take stock of your personality characteristics. Are you more impulsive than most? Do you think about the consequences of your actions before you dive in head first? Are you attracted to thrilling new adventures more than most? Are you hyperactive? Can you identify with Childhood Conduct Disorder symptoms? Do you think your personality characteristics have fueled your drinking?

Family Influences

You learned a lot about drinking and alcohol from your parent's example. You learned how to drink, when to drink and why to drink from them. You learned their beliefs and expectations about drinking and alcohol too.

If you grew up in a household that misused booze, most likely you inherited problem drinking habits and attitudes. During your formative years, you picked up your parent's bad behaviors, beliefs and attitudes about liquor and made them your own. And unfortunately, the old problem drinking thinking and patterns you learned as a kid are probably still with you today. In fact, women drinkers seem to be more susceptible to family influence when it comes to drinking and alcohol than men.

Your relationship with your parents may have shaped your current drinking patterns too. The quality of communication and involvement you had with them when you were growing up may have factored in. If you had a healthy, involved relationship with your parents and felt comfortable communicating your thoughts and feelings to them, the less you needed to escape or rebel with beer. But if you lived in an unhealthy family atmosphere that discouraged open communication, you may have used beer to break away and revolt.

Did you inherit bad drinking habits, attitudes, beliefs and expectations about drinking and alcohol from your parents? Did liquor flow freely in your house? Did your parents drink often? Did one or both of your parents have a drinking problem? Did you ever see one or both of your parents get drunk? Did they get drunk often? Was your relationship with your parents good, bad or indifferent? How did your relationship with your parents affect your current drinking behavior?

Childhood Abuse and Trauma

If you were sexually, physically or emotionally abused or had a traumatic experience as a child, you're at greater your risk for problem drinking. You're more likely to drink, get intoxicated and have alcohol-related problems. And the more adverse your experiences were, the higher your odds are of becoming dependent on booze in adulthood.

Childhood sexual abuse is the single strongest predictor of alcohol addiction in women! More than two-thirds of alcohol-abusing women seeking treatment have suffered some form of childhood sexual abuse, compared to one-third of women in the general population.

But childhood sexual abuse isn't the only type of mistreatment that can lead to problem drinking in women. Females who were emotionally or physically harmed as children are also more inclined to misuse alcohol. The hurt that a woman has endured as a child often stays with her and remains unresolved, so she hits the bottle to ease her pain.

In addition to hard drinking, childhood abuse survivors may also struggle with Post Traumatic Stress Disorder - PTSD - an anxiety disorder that develops in some people who've had extremely disturbing experiences. Symptoms include frightening nightmares, hallucinations, flashbacks, irritability, angry outbursts, difficulty concentrating, insomnia and an exaggerated startle response. Individuals suffering from

PTSD become so anxious that their lives become disrupted and they avoid anything that reminds them of their awful experiences. And they may rely on liquor to relieve these feelings and symptoms which can result in alcohol dependence.

A traumatic event in childhood, like the death of a parent, a serious illness or living in extreme poverty, may also lead to unhealthy drinking. Living with sadness and loss, never properly grieving or trying to cope with a stressful event when you're young may have started you drinking early and kept you drinking.

Were you a victim of sexual, physical or emotional abuse when you were a child? Did you suffer a traumatic event in your childhood that still haunts you today? Do you have unresolved feelings about the abuse or trauma? Do you use alcohol to cope with these feelings?

Traditional Roles

Have you always strived to be the perfect daughter, wife and mother? Have you ever struggled to fulfill traditional women's roles? Have you ever been confused about your identity, roles and responsibilities as a woman? Have you ever resented, rejected or rebelled against the roles you were born into? If you've ever questioned your female identity or roles, if you feel you can't keep up with all of the expectations and obligations of your roles or if you resent and reject traditional roles that were handed to you, you may be drinking to maintain.

Women who don't go with the flow and denounce defined social roles have higher rates of alcohol abuse. On the one hand, the more roles a woman can identify with, the stronger her self-esteem is and the more support she enjoys, which combined with increased responsibility, discourages problem drinking. But on the other hand, if a woman dislikes, is confused by or can barely cope with all of the traditional roles assigned to her, she might turn to wine to get by.

Daughter, wife, mother, homemaker, caregiver, nurturer. There's not enough time in the day for a woman to keep up with all that's expected of her. But one thing is certain - alcohol abuse doesn't fit into any one of these roles. Society is disgusted by a drunk woman and women who drink heavily are not only thought to be sexually aggressive and promiscuous, they're also considered failures as partners and mothers too. Just the opposite of what a lady is supposed to be.

Your dislike, confusion or rejection of how you should behave as a female may start early. And even though peer pressure is the number one reason behind most teenage girl's drinking, trying to live up to the feminine ideal you may have been raised with can also figure in. Being the perfect woman, wife and mother - pretty, nice, smart, submissive, supportive and putting everyone else first and yourself last - can be a tall order for many young women. So drinking to rebel against these traditional identities, roles and expectations might happen.

When you become a wife or partner, you're expected to be loving and loyal at all cost. You're also expected to be passive, conforming, unselfish and nurturing. The feminine ideal in most cultures always thinks of others first and is not expected to express anger or sadness. In fact, you're supposed to suppress all negative feelings.

Making a comfortable home, encouraging and supporting your significant other and raising kids are your main functions. You're a good listener and the perfect wife - attractive, a good cook and meticulous housekeeper. You work hard to make your family happy and keep the household running smoothly.

As a mother you're expected to love your children unconditionally. Mothers are the keepers of relationships and supposed to be more virtuous and caring than men. You're everything to everyone and if you drink in excess you probably feel ashamed and guilty about it. You might hate yourself for it and feel you've failed your children. You might think you're a bad parent and role model. And these feelings may be exacerbated if you work outside of the home.

So many roles for women these days, so little time. It's hard enough to take on all of women's traditional roles and expectations and try to make everyone happy. But when you combine them with being the breadwinner and the head of the household, it's even harder. And the pressures and responsibilities of so many roles and expectations mount - creating stress and conflict that can trigger problem drinking.

Have you ever questioned, disliked, rejected or been confused by your roles as a woman? Do you suppress your feelings to fulfill your roles and expectations? Does juggling all of your roles drive you to drink? Do you use alcohol to help you manage your roles and all of the responsibilities they entail?

Relationships

Relationships may be at the core of your drinking problem. Difficult or unresolved dealings with parents, partners, kids, friends and colleagues may push your buttons and you may use liquor to cope. Or as a tool to speak your mind or to obtain love, power, control or intimacy in a relationship.

Maybe your connection with your parents still drives you crazy. If you were starved for their affection when you were young, odds are you're still trying to win it today. If, on the other hand, you were the apple of their eye, the world was expected of you and you feel you failed them, you're probably still trying to prove yourself to them. If your parents put you down when you were a kid, you're most likely trying to show them and the world you're somebody. If they abused you, you might hate them for it and turned to drugs and alcohol to get back at them. Or perhaps your parents divorced and remarried and you don't get along with their partners, so you hit the bottle to handle the situation. So many different dysfunctional parent/child scenarios are possible. And the satisfaction or dissatisfaction you feel about yourself and your life today may be the direct or indirect result of the relationship you had with your parents - and influencing your drinking today.

You may use spirits to try and find love or to start a relationship. You think it makes you more attractive and outgoing. You feel less inhibited and more aggressive when you're under the influence. You think it helps you to emotionally connect with potential partners too. Having a few cocktails makes you more fun and sexier - you think.

If you're happy in a romantic relationship, you might use liquor to enhance it. You and your mate enjoy drinking together and you think it brings you closer together. Or you drink for the approval of your mate. Or you use booze as an aphrodisiac - to increase your sexual desire or pleasure. Drinking with your partner may seal the relationship deal for both of you.

If you're unhappy in a romantic relationship, you might use a martini to try to connect and communicate. Or to fix problems you're having. Drinking may be the only enjoyable activity you share with your mate. It might help you to tolerate the relationship. Or to control your partner. Or your partner might use it to control you. It might be a tool for you or your mate to gain more power in the relationship.

Heavy drinkers tend to marry heavy drinkers. And a partner who abuses alcohol increases your chances of abusing alcohol. Hard drinking in a relationship also increases your chances of being physically, emotionally and/or verbally abused. Women in treatment for alcoholism are four times more likely to be victims of domestic abuse.

Relationships with your kids might be driving you nuts too. If your children are on the right path, lucky you. But kids will be kids and that means questioning authority, experimenting and rebelling against you and society. Keeping your cool during the ups and downs of parenting and not resorting to liquor may be one of the biggest challenges of your life.

Your kids may judge you and put you down for your drinking. They may be embarrassed by your drinking. They may blame you and your drinking for their problems. And you may overcompensate to make up for your drinking problem. You may be too permissive and overindulge them because you know you drink too much. You may allow them to engage in unacceptable behavior, but you don't step in because you feel guilty about your excessive drinking.

You may neglect your kids when you're drinking. Or you may be cruel to them when you're drinking. Or you may drink with them to communicate and bond - in an attempt to mend your relationship. When women fail children because of alcohol, the guilt and shame they feel is enormous - eroding their self-esteem even further which can lead to even more drinking.

Complicated family structures and dynamics may also be getting to you. Blended families and child custody conditions and arrangements may be making your life miserable. Traditional families have their problems, but complex blended families can be even more demanding.

Connections with friends and colleagues may also figure into your desire to drink. Meaningful relationships sometimes involve conflict and change. And working through these tough times can make a friendship even stronger. But you may take the easy way out and tipple instead.

Has your relationship with your parents shaped your alcohol use? Do you use liquor to look for love or to cultivate a romantic relationship? Do you drink with or without your partner? How does booze factor into your relationship with your mate? Does your drinking add or detract from it? Do kids drive you to drink? How do spirits fit into your relationship with your children? Is your drinking an issue for your friends or colleagues? Do relationship issues trip your alcohol appetite and overdrinking?

Low Self-Esteem

Low self-esteem is a strong predictor of alcohol abuse among women. And the bottom line is when you don't think you're the greatest, you may drink to feel better about yourself.

Maybe you're unhappy with your body. Many women define themselves by their appearance. Maybe you're obsessed with your weight. Or you hate your nose, lips, stomach or some other body part. If your body image falls short, your self-esteem and self-confidence may also fall short. And you might drink to forget about your flaws.

Low self-esteem may be a reflection of the state of your relationships and how you see yourself socially too. If you have unhealthy relationships and you feel mistreated, you don't feel valued by others so you don't value yourself. If you're not popular or don't have many friends, you might not feel you deserve good friends. Your self-esteem can also take a hit if you think you haven't achieved a certain social status. If you're unhappy because you're not the belle of the ball or the leader of the pack, you might think you don't measure up and you may use booze to deal with these feelings.

If you don't think you're the world's greatest wife, mother, homemaker, professional or moneymaker, you may think less of yourself. Most of us have been pressured from an early age to excel at everything. And most of us miss the mark at times. So when we set the bar too high and don't live up to our great expectations, we're disappointed. And we might drink our disillusionment away.

Using beer to feel better about yourself can start early. A typical young woman is concerned about being pretty, popular with her peers and establishing her own identity while conforming to her social group. And when you add sex and romantic relationships to the mix, it's clear a young woman has a lot on her plate. And robust self-worth seems almost impossible to attain. Unfortunately, teenage girls with weak self-esteem are twice as likely to abuse alcohol than girls with strong self-esteem.

Low self-esteem can affect college women's alcohol use too. College women are still struggling with all of the feelings they had as a teenager, but now they're facing the added pressures of assuming adult roles and responsibilities, like getting married, establishing a career and making something of themselves. And sex, romantic relationships and academic and professional achievements are even more important to them during this time. If they feel they're not good enough - physically, intellectually, academically, socially, financially or professionally - and they're shouldering the weight of new adult obligations, spirits may be an attractive escape. It's a convenient and socially acceptable way to feel better about yourself fast. College women who report having a drinking problem are four times more likely to report feelings of worthlessness compared to college women who do not report having a drinking problem.

If you're between thirty and fifty years old, your life may revolve around relationships and motherhood and you might base your self-worth on them. So if your marriage isn't working or your kids are acting up, you blame yourself. In fact, you probably take the blame for all failed relationships - romantic, marital and parental. And if your relationships fail, you fail, your self-esteem plummets and you drink to pump yourself up. Problem drinking women are twenty-five times more likely to feel like failures in their roles of wife, mother and nurturer than women who don't drink problematically.

If you're over fifty, your self-esteem is probably tied to your past accomplishments. So if you look at your life and your achievements and like what you see, you feel good about yourself. But if you look at your life and see mistakes and missed opportunities, you don't feel good about yourself and you could be drinking to soothe those negative feelings.

Do you dislike your body? Do you feel you don't measure up - physically, intellectually, academically, socially, financially or professionally? Does low self-esteem spark your alcohol appetite? Do you drink to make up for bad feelings you have about yourself?

Depression

Depression is the most commonly diagnosed psychiatric disorder among alcoholic women. If you're sad or unhappy and think you have little or no control over your life, you may be depressed. If you have no energy or interest in living, you no longer enjoy family, friends or activities you use to enjoy, you feel tired often, you have headaches, stomachaches or backaches often, you can't sleep or sleep too much or you can't eat or eat too much, you're experiencing symptoms of depression. If you're unable to concentrate or make decisions, you feel anxious or guilty often, you're preoccupied with death and dying or you're rebellious, promiscuous or irresponsible at times, take note because these are also signs of depression.

One in four women suffers from depression at some time in their life and it's usually caused by a combination of genetic, chemical, biological, psychological, social or environmental factors. Women seem to be more sensitive to their emotions and relationships than men which may predispose them to it.

Many depressed women medicate with liquor which is not a great idea because alcohol abuse can actually exacerbate depression. So if you drink heavily when you're depressed, you can fall into an even deeper depression.

Can you relate to any symptoms of depression? Do you drink - or overdrink - to treat your depression?

Stress

Stress can play a big role in a woman's drinking. If you feel tense, pressured, overworked or overwhelmed, you might be stressed out. Anxiety, agitation, always thinking you have too much to do, not being able to concentrate, not being able to relax after you've fulfilled your obligations, not enjoying people or activities you use to enjoy and sleeping problems are also common symptoms of stress. Feeling angry, down, tired, on edge, having headaches or stomachaches and feeling overloaded and over stimulated are stress symptoms too.

Women stress over everything and tend to hold it in, compared to men. We overthink our problems and constantly analyze the meanings and ramifications of our actions. But this overthinking and overanalyzing just leads to more stress.

Women also tend to wait out a problem - a stressor. We hope it will improve or fade away over time. And we turn inward and to alcohol while we're waiting. So instead of trying to fix the stressor causing our tension in a healthy way, we try to fix our inner self with liquor in an unhealthy way. Simply put, women try to manage their stress with booze. Unfortunately, when you hit the bottle to cope with stress, problem drinking isn't far behind.

Can you relate to any symptoms associated with stress? Do you drink - or overdrink - when you're stressed out? Do you overthink or overanalyze your problems - stressing yourself out even more? Do you patiently wait for problems to resolve themselves with a drink in your hand? Or do you address a stressor head on and try to fix it?

Feelings, Moods and Mental Health Conditions

Many women lean on liquor to treat feelings, moods or mental health conditions. Some women drink to lift their spirits. Some drink to calm down. Some drink because they're happy. Some drink because they're sad. Some drink because they're satisfied. Some drink to feel powerful. Some drink to feel in control. Some drink to cope. Some drink to feel hopeful. Some drink to take the edge off of loneliness. Some drink to entertain themselves. And some drink to fill a void in their life.

Mental health conditions may also influence a woman's drinking. Anxiety is a common problem that can lead to alcohol abuse. If you're suffering from anxiety, you feel worried, tense and nervous often. You can't stop worrying and you worry most of the time. You worry when you have no good reason to worry. You worry about everyday activities. Your worry is unrealistic and exaggerated. You may also feel fearful, irritable, tired, and restless, you may have difficulty concentrating, trouble eating or sleeping, you may suffer from headaches or muscle tension or you may sweat and tremble at times. You may have panic attacks and startle easily. Anxiety dominates your thinking and your life and you may use vodka to relieve it.

Adult Deficit Hyperactivity Disorder, ADHD, can also result in problem drinking. Symptoms include hyperactivity, difficulty controlling your behavior, having a hard time staying focused or paying attention, getting bored easily, feeling restless or agitated, craving excitement often, being into risk taking, being reckless and spontaneous at times without thinking of the consequences, having trouble behaving appropriately in social situations, talking over others, frequently interrupting others, having poor self-control or blurting out thoughts that are rude or inappropriate. And you may treat yourself with vodka to slow down.

Bipolar Disorder, which is a serious mental health illness where common emotions become intense and unpredictable, can also lead to risky drinking. You might have mood swings from one extreme to another. You might be happy and energetic one minute and sad, tired and confused the next. You may even feel suicidal at times. People suffering from this condition all have manic episodes where they become abnormally happy or irritable that last at least a week, but not all bipolar people become depressed. If you suffer from bipolar disorder, booze may be your drug of choice - mellowing you out when you're excited and raising you up when you're down.

What feelings trigger your desire to drink and overdrinking? When you're up, do you drink to feel even better? When you're down, do you drink to pick yourself up? Does your mood determine your alcohol consumption? Do you think you suffer from a mental health condition that fuels your drinking? Do you use alcohol to treat anxiety, ADHD or Bipolar Disorder?

Peer Pressure

Women of all ages may drink to belong. Peer pressure is more strongly associated with drinking for girls than it is for boys. Teenage girls desperately wanting to be accepted and popular may binge drink. College women who belong to sororities are much more likely to drink than women who do not belong to sororities. Women in their thirties and forties drink to keep up with their friends and so they won't feel left out. And middle-aged and older women imbibe because their partners, friends or acquaintances drink and they feel they have to join in.

How old were you when you took your first drink? What were the circumstances? Did your friends coerce you into drinking when you were young? Today, do you drink to fit in, make friends or be popular? Do you think peer pressure factors in to your current drinking behavior?

Life Transitions

Big changes in your life may be responsible for your alcohol intake. When you're young, leaving home, starting college or a new job, breaking up with a boyfriend, having an unwanted pregnancy, the death of a parent or loved one or your parents splitting up may be to blame for your drinking.

During your early adult and middle years a crisis - an affair, a miscarriage, a divorce or a child leaving home - may be behind your drinking. Employment problems, financial concerns and changes in the family structure can also lead to drinking.

When you're a senior, major upsets may trip your heavy drinking. Retirement, empty nest syndrome, the death of a spouse, relative or friend, a sudden or chronic illness, employment or money problems, loneliness, boredom, poor social support or loss of independent living may result in drinking.

Did your drinking become a problem when you were facing a transition in your life? What changed? Were there two or more big shifts happening at the same time? What were they? Are you currently drinking too much to deal with an upsetting event? Or have you survived a change in your life, but still drinking heavily?

Filling the Void

Many women drink during times of lack or loss - the ending of a relationship, not having a relationship, not having a job, suffering a miscarriage, being widowed, getting divorced, having children leave home or feeling that they've been abandoned. They hit the bottle because they have poor coping skills and they use liquor to make up for the emptiness.

Again, women tend to wait and hope things will get better when times are tough. But they often wait with a glass in their hand and drink more than women who have better coping skills.

Have you experienced a loss in your life recently? What was it? Or did your loss happen years ago, but you're still in the same heavy drinking pattern you developed to deal with it way back when? Do you use alcohol to fill the hole inside of you?

Workplace Stress

For the most part, working women do not have higher alcohol abuse rates than non-working women and there is no correlation between a woman's employment status and alcoholism. But women who work in male-dominated professions, like engineering or finance, drink more and are more likely to have problems with booze than women who work in predominantly female-dominated professions, like teaching or nursing.

Women do not tend to drink because of work-related stress. Yet sixty-seven percent of women who work outside of the home are more likely to drink heavily than homemakers. Perhaps they drink more in response to increased responsibilities - managing the family and household affairs in addition to working.

Employed single women are more likely to develop alcohol problems than employed married women. Single women seem to use spirits to cope with job stress. They engage in escapist drinking - drinking to relax after work or to forget about problems at work. And single women with both work and home demands have higher rates of alcohol abuse in general.

Do you rely on wine to handle workplace stress? Do you unwind after work with a cocktail or two or three? When you're under the gun at work, do you drink more? What effect does job pressure have on your alcohol consumption?

Expectations and Beliefs About Alcohol

Your expectations and beliefs about alcohol may predict how much and how often you drink. Many women believe liquor will have a positive effect on them - easing tension, enhancing a good mood or elevating a bad one. So naturally, if you expect wine will make you feel better, the more you'll drink.

Girls who drink heavily are more likely than boys who drink heavily to use booze to escape their problems and to manage depression, anger, frustration and stress. They believe it's a tool to deal with downer emotions and states of mind. Young women also believe alcohol will make them more desirable and assertive, while decreasing their social anxiety.

Women who drink to treat sadness or depression report more alcohol use than those who don't report these problems. Again, they hold an underlying belief in the positive power of spirits to deal with unwanted feelings. Women may also have higher expectations than men about liquor's ability to enhance sexual pleasure. Ironically, women's sexual arousal and ability to achieve orgasm actually decrease the more they drink.

Unhealthy, unrealistic beliefs and expectations about drinking and alcohol may include the more you drink, the better you'll feel. Or that wine will make you more likeable and popular. You may think liquor will make it easier for you to make friends or start a romantic relationship.

You may expect to feel sexier and believe you're more desirable when you're under the influence. Or that drinking is an expression of your individuality and bingeing is a good way to rebel. Or that beer will help you to cope with feelings and problems. Risky and irrational attitudes about booze.

Healthy, realistic beliefs and expectations about drinking and alcohol, on the other hand, should include that liquor can make you happy - but only temporarily. It can also make you feel better about yourself and raise your self-esteem - but only temporarily. It can increase your self-confidence - but only temporarily. A little wine can be a social lubricant and may make you feel a bit more relaxed and friendlier in social settings. A little wine may make you feel less inhibited and more open to a romantic relationship. But a margarita will not initiate or maintain meaningful relationships. Drinking is not an appropriate expression of your individuality or an effective way to rebel. More alcohol is not better. It will just make you silly and sick. And spirits will not resolve any of your problems or improve your mood long-term. Safe and rational attitudes about booze.

What are your unrealistic beliefs and expectations about alcohol? What are your realistic beliefs and expectations about alcohol? How do you expect to feel about yourself, your problems and your life after a cocktail or two? How do you expect to feel about yourself, your problems and your life after too many cocktails? Does alcohol really live up to your beliefs and expectations?

Other Risk Factors

Your age, marital status, if you have children, your employment status and your cultural background may all play into your drinking. Women at greatest risk for problem drinking are in their thirties and forties, divorced, childless or have no children living at home and are unemployed. And you're less at risk if you're married and employed full-time.

Generally, women under forty drink more than women over forty and women over fifty tend to drink even less and heavy drinking drops dramatically. But women in their fifties and sixties who are unemployed and have no children at home are more likely to abuse alcohol than their counterparts who are employed and have children at home.

Heavy drinking rates are higher among divorced women and women who have never been married. And women who live with a partner, but have never married, have the highest risk of developing a drinking problem. In fact, women who are not married but live with a partner are fifty percent more likely to drink heavily than married women. Widows also have a high risk of developing a drinking problem.

Problem drinking women get together with problem drinking men. And your partner can play a role in your drinking. They can encourage it, discourage it, ignore it or use it as a tool to control you or the relationship. An unhappy relationship or marriage can drive you to drink. But a happy relationship or marriage can protect you and reduce your chances of abusing alcohol.

In general, white women are in greater danger of drinking problematically than Hispanic women. And African American women are the least likely to have drinking problems, compared to other ethnic and racial groups. Cultural attitudes you grow up with can shape your drinking habits.

Do you think your age, marital status, having children or not having children, employment status, ethnic or cultural background have figured into your drinking? For better or for worse?

What's Your Story?

When you pinpoint the underlying issues in your life that have led to your drinking, the more insight and understanding you'll have about it. And the easier it will be for you to let go of your unhealthy drinking habits and replace them with healthy new ones.

Now it's time for you to write your own story - when, where, why and how you became so interested in alcohol. So dig deep and examine all of the issues and problems in your past and present that have driven you to drink. Then write your story.

What started you drinking? Maybe you began in response to some sort of sexual, emotional or physical abuse or trauma you suffered as a child. Or you learned your heavy drinking ways from your parents. Maybe you didn't get the support you needed when you were growing up and you drank to rebel. Perhaps cultural attitudes about drinking and liquor are responsible for your drinking habits. Maybe you inherited a biological or genetic predisposition for alcohol abuse. There could be a million different reasons why you picked up the bottle in the first place.

Maybe you got into booze because of the company you kept. You binged when you were young because all of your friends binged. Or you started drinking after work with colleagues to blow off steam and it became a ritual. Or you partied throughout high school and college, continued to drink through marriage and motherhood and never outgrew your hard drinking ways. And alcohol-abusing pals and socially acceptable excuses have kept your problem drinking alive and well.

Maybe you turned to wine to help you live up to your roles and obligations. Being a partner. Being a mother. Being a professional woman. Being the breadwinner. Being the head of the household. Staying at home. Working outside of the home. Or working and raising kids at the same time. So many choices. If you've ever been conflicted about your identity and duties or you've assumed too much responsibility at home or work and you use liquor to see you through, now's the time for you to get your feelings off your chest and onto paper.

How have relationships factored into your problem drinking equation? If you're unhappy, this is your opportunity to vent. If your parents, partner, kids, friends or colleagues are making you crazy, express yourself. Recognizing how relationships affect your drinking is crucial to your self-examination and your story.

Maybe you started relying on booze to treat feelings, moods or a mental health condition. Depression or feeling stuck may have started you drinking. Or anxiety, ADHD or Bipolar Disorder triggered it. Don't underestimate the power that emotions, moods or mental health issues can have on your drinking behavior.

If low self-esteem and a lack of self-confidence have influenced your alcohol intake, stop sweeping them under the rug. If you don't value or feel sure about yourself, you're more likely to have a substance abuse problem. Admit it, then you can get past it.

Maybe you drank heavily at different times in your life. Perhaps alcohol was becoming an issue for you in your high school or college years. Maybe you outgrew it. Maybe not. Perhaps it was becoming more important to you when you were raising your kids - in your thirties and forties. And it escalated when they moved out of the house. Maybe your golden years are becoming your problem drinking years. What else is there to do?

What issues and problems have affected your drinking? Be honest with yourself and the more specific you are, the better. Get busy writing your story right now. It's the starting point of your healthy new drinking habits and life!

Step Two

Demystify Your Drinking

∞ *Chapter 3* ∞

What's Your Drinking Style?

Your drinking style is the distinctive way you drink. Do you binge - drinking fast and furious - like an adolescent? Have you fallen into a drinking habit - engaging in the same old drinking rut almost every day? Do you drink when you're stressed - using liquor to relax? Or do you drink in response to emotional ups and downs - downing booze to treat your feelings?

There are four common drinking styles and most of us don't adhere to just one exclusively. In fact, most of us can identify with at least two, maybe three or even all four of them. But there is one that you engage in more often and that's your dominant drinking style. The others are your secondary drinking styles.

Recognizing all of the different ways you drink is necessary for several reasons. First, you have to know what your drinking styles are before you can change them. Second, when you become aware of your specific styles, you'll be less susceptible to them. You'll know exactly what's happening and you'll no longer take part in mindless drinking. And third, the more thoughtful you are about your problem drinking styles, the less you'll drink naturally!

Binge Drinking

When you drink, do you guzzle? Do you get smashed almost every time you drink? Do you blackout frequently and have a hard time remembering the party the next day? You're a binge drinker.

Binge drinking is consuming a large quantity of alcohol and usually getting drunk. Maybe you don't even drink that often, but when you do, you gulp your drinks in record time and get wasted. That's binge drinking.

Binge drinking is a common drinking style for younger drinkers and many people outgrow it. But if you haven't outgrown it, address it now because it's one of the most dangerous problem drinking styles. When you binge, you could die from alcohol poisoning, you're more likely to hurt or kill yourself or someone else, you're at greater risk of sexual and physical assaults and you're more sexually active. You're totally out of control and you say and do things you would never dream of saying and doing if you hadn't binged. You're an accident just waiting to happen.

Maybe you were a binge drinker when you were young - in your teen or college years - and you've moved past it. Maybe you still binge occasionally - when you're under pressure or with other binge drinkers. Or maybe binge drinking is your primary drinking style and it happens most every time you imbibe. If you've engaged in binge drinking over the last year, record it on a drinking style list.

Habitual Drinking

Do you usually drink every day - most often at the same time, the same place and have about the same number of drinks? Do you head for the fridge or liquor cabinet as soon as you get home and automatically pour yourself a cocktail? Or do you go out for drinks everyday after work? Does your happy hour last at least two or three hours everyday? Does nothing come between you and your toddy? It's a daily ritual and you plan your day around it? You're a habitual drinker.

Even though you may stop at three or four glasses and you don't get wild and crazy, you're still drinking too much. Plus, you've built up a tolerance to alcohol in addition to forming a nasty habit. Just think of the long-term health problems caused by habitual drinking - pounding your body with vodka day after day. Yes, the toll daily drinking is taking on your body is bad, but the psychological toll may be even worse. You feel hooked on liquor. It's become a monkey on your back. And you might even feel you're becoming addicted to it.

If your body and soul have been paying the price for a drinking habit within the last year, add it to your drinking style list.

Stress-Related Drinking

Are you dying for a drink after a rough day? When you're stressed about work, money, relationships or life, do you drink? When you're under pressure, do you hit the bottle? You're a stress-related drinker.

Stress-related drinkers use alcohol to get through tough times. But, in fact, drinking in excess to manage stress usually backfires. When you drink heavily, you don't feel one-hundred percent physically or mentally - which makes it even more difficult for you to deal with it. And eventually, you become stressed about your drinking too. So instead of lightening your load, you actually add to it when you abuse alcohol.

If liquor is your stress reduction strategy of choice and you've engaged in this problem drinking style over the last year, add it to your drinking style list.

Emotional Drinking

Do you drink when you're up? To make good times even better? Do you drink when you're down? To improve your mood if you're sad, lonely, angry or frustrated? Do you use spirits to enhance positive feelings or to numb negative ones or both? You're an emotional drinker.

When your feelings are getting the best of you, you bring out the booze. You pour yourself a martini when you hit a roadblock or you down a margarita to party even harder. But overdrinking to elevate or enhance your emotions doesn't really work. It just deadens you and prevents you from truly enjoying positive feelings or dealing with negative ones.

If you guzzle when you're high or low or both and you've engaged in emotional problem drinking within the last year, add it to your drinking style list.

What's Your Drinking Style?

What's your dominant drinking style? Are you a binge drinker, habitual drinker, stress-related or emotional drinker most of the time? What are your secondary drinking styles? Do you binge occasionally? Do you overdo it when you're stressed? Do you get bombed when you close a big deal? Do you bring out the bottle when you're fighting with your significant other?

Identify and record all of your drinking styles. Soon, you'll challenge each and every one of them!

∽ Chapter 4 ∽

What's Your Drinking Pattern?

Your drinking pattern is the way you organize your life around alcohol. Do you use play dates, book clubs or game nights as excuses to drink? Do you drink with your partner and family because you rationalize that it brings you closer together? Do you sneak a glass of wine after the kids are in bed or before your mate gets home? Do you have a cocktail after work and drink your way through dinner? Do you give yourself a free pass to drink all you want on weekends? Do you drink in secret?

Most likely, you can relate to more than one drinking pattern and drinking patterns may change at different times in your life. And your age, social class, economic status, occupation and lifestyle may all have some effect on them. Also, like drinking styles, you probably have a dominant drinking pattern - one that you engage in more frequently - and secondary ones that you engage in less frequently.

Understanding your drinking patterns is just as important as understanding your drinking styles. Once you're aware of them, you can change them for the better. You'll no longer drink mindlessly. And you'll drink less automatically!

Teenage Girl's Drinking Patterns

When you're a teenager you're evolving from a girl into a young woman, an adult - a difficult transition. Your body is changing. Your social life is changing. Your attitudes and goals are changing. And your duties and responsibilities are changing. In fact, your whole world is changing. Your body image, making new friends, having an active social life, excelling academically and pleasing others are probably high on your list of priorities. Not to mention a newfound interest in romantic relationships and sex. You're curious and into new experiences too. And experimenting with alcohol is one of them.

The seeds of your current drinking pattern may have been sown during your teen years. Maybe you snuck your first drink at home when your parents were away. Or you binged with friends. They encouraged you to get drunk and you went along with it. Peer pressure to drink and fit in is huge during the teen years. Maybe drinking made you feel better about yourself - increasing your self-esteem and self-confidence. Maybe you felt so pressured by your parents to do well you swilled beer to blow off steam. Or you used it as a weapon to rebel against them, school and society. Perhaps you only drank on Fridays or the weekends. Or only with certain buddies. Or only when you went clubbing. Or secretly behind the barn. Common drinking patterns for young people.

What drinking patterns did you learn as a young person? Are you still into problem drinking patterns you picked up as a teenager? What are they? If you've engaged in any one of these adolescent drinking patterns over the last year, record it on a drinking pattern list.

College Women's Drinking Patterns

Peer pressure and the need for you to succeed become even more intense in college. And assuming your adult identity, taking on even more responsibilities, establishing long-term meaningful relationships, achieving your academic goals and proving yourself are at the forefront during these years.

Your drinking pattern during this time may have included drinking only on weekends or Fridays and Saturdays or at parties and sporting events. You may have competed in drinking games - like beer pong or jello shots. Drinking and getting smashed were rites of passage - especially if you belonged to a sorority. Keg parties were popular - especially after finals. And spring break was one big alcoholic blowout. Maybe you dieted and drank - risky because drinking on an empty stomach exaggerates the effects of alcohol. All common drinking patterns for college students.

What drinking patterns did you develop in college? Are you still stuck in them today? If you've engaged in any one of these college drinking patterns over the last year, add it to your drinking pattern list.

Young and Middle-Age Women's Drinking Patterns

Between the ages of thirty and fifty many women drink to deal with relationships, marriage and motherhood - and all of the added responsibilities that these roles entail. Fitting wine into your busy schedule can be a challenge, but you get creative and label almost any occasion a drinking occasion. You also know that drinking in excess is socially unacceptable for women, wives and mothers, so to keep up appearances you go out of your way to rationalize or hide your drinking. The last thing you want is to be branded a loose woman or an unfit mother because you drink too much.

If you're in a relationship with a heavy drinking partner, you might drink together to connect. You and your problem drinking spouse both abuse alcohol so you don't judge or criticize each other's drinking. Hard drinking is the norm. Besides, you're not sure if you want to rock the boat - as far as booze and your relationship are concerned. You think you might be jeopardizing the union if you start questioning your drinking or your drinking patterns together.

You might go overboard in social situations. You look forward to parties, get-togethers, book clubs, charity functions, sporting events, weddings and family reunions to justify your heavy drinking. Game nights with the girls might be your favorite outings. And bunko and sex toy parties always have liquor flowing. The best part is nobody's keeping an eye on how much you're having at these functions because your pals are getting wasted too.

Girl's night out might be your excuse to binge. And if you and the ladies vacation together, getting plastered may be half the fun. What happens in Vegas stays in Vegas. Let's not forget about play date drinking with other moms! The kids can have their fun and you can have yours too. Or calling friends after a couple of margaritas might be your thing. You enjoy dialing drunk. You have fascinating conversations and get caught up when you're under the influence.

You might go underground and engage in secret drinking. Drinking when no one's home. Or sneaking off into another room for a nip when others are around. You might tipple before the mate or kids get home. Or you might have bottles stashed all over the house in case of an emergency.

Maybe you do most of your drinking at home. You might start when you're making dinner - an excellent reason to open a bottle. And you drink your way through your meal and the rest of the evening until you go to bed. You might drink when you're doing boring household chores to liven things up. Or you start drinking after the kids are tucked in. That way they never see their mom getting tanked.

You may drink to get out of your rut. You may drink to give yourself a break from kids and mothering. You may drink because you're bored. You may drink because you're lonely. You may drink to relieve stress or depression. Whatever your reasons, you always manage to get your cocktails in.

Did your drinking become an issue for you in adulthood? Have the pressures and responsibilities of your roles, relationships or motherhood driven you to drink? What drinking patterns have you developed as an adult? If you've engaged in any one of these young and middle-age women's drinking patterns over the last year, add it to your drinking pattern list.

Older Women's Drinking Patterns

Older women often drink at home alone or with other seniors who have a fondness for alcohol. If you're retired and have time on your hands, you might fill it with wine. Or if you're bored, you might entertain yourself with vodka. Or if you socialize with hard drinking friends, you and tequila always join the party.

Empty nest syndrome, the death of a spouse, family member or friend, health problems and financial crises can all contribute to older women's drinking. Loneliness and monotony may also factor in. Booze might take the edge off of the anxiety you feel about the future too. Or fill a void in your life. When you're high, you feel full, not empty. Or you drink because you think your life is over and you might as well have a stiff one.

Has alcohol abuse become a concern for you in your later years? Has a feeling of loss, loneliness or emptiness crept over you - increasing your desire to drink? What problem drinking patterns have you developed as an older adult? If you've engaged in any one of these drinking patterns over the last year, add it to your drinking pattern list.

What Are Your Drinking Patterns?

What's your dominant drinking pattern? Are you still guzzling like a teenager? Are you stuck in your college drinking pattern? Are game nights and play dates your downfalls? Do you drink alone or with other seniors? What are your secondary drinking patterns?

Identify and record all of your drinking patterns. Once you've figured them out, you can take them on and be rid of them!

Step Three

Jumpstart Your Healthy New Drinking Habits

Chapter 5

Lay Your Moderate Drinking Foundation

Y ou'll build your sensible drinking behavior from the ground up. First, you'll find out exactly what moderate drinking is, make your commitment to change and get acquainted with the Drink/Link Change Your Drinking Behavior Formula. Then you'll set your drink limits and learn five safe-drinking guidelines, the Drink/Link Basics. Finally, you'll discover how to motivate yourself to stick to the program and reward yourself for a job well done.

Take your time and allow yourself at least one week - longer if you like - to digest all the information in this chapter. You want to lay a sturdy foundation for healthy drinking habits you'll enjoy for the rest of your life!

What is Moderate Drinking?

It's reasonable, problem-free drinking that doesn't cause any health, psychological, relationship, social, school, work, legal or financial problems for you or anyone else. Moderate drinking complements your life, it isn't your life.

The United States Dietary Guidelines for Americans, issued jointly by the United States Departments of Agriculture and Health and Human Services, considers moderate drinking for women one drink a day and up to seven drinks per week. Light drinking for women is up to three drinks a week and heavy drinking is fourteen or more drinks per week. Remember - a woman metabolizes alcohol differently than a man and gets higher on the same amount than a man. That's why only one drink a day is considered moderate drinking for a woman, compared to two drinks a day for a man.

Problem drinking or alcohol abuse is drinking that's harmful to you or others. If you get drunk or have hangovers often, if you miss school or work or skip child care responsibilities because of drinking, if you drink in situations that can be dangerous, such as drinking before or during driving, if you have legal problems because of your drinking, like being arrested when you're under the influence, and if you continue to drink even though you have ongoing alcohol-related problems, you're a problem drinker.

And alcoholism or alcohol dependence is even more serious than problem drinking and can be life threatening. If you have alcohol cravings - a strong need or compulsion to drink, if you have no control over your drinking and you're unable to stop once you've started, if you're physically dependent on alcohol and suffer from withdrawal symptoms when you don't drink - you get nauseated, sweat, shake, become irritable and anxious, if you've developed a high tolerance to alcohol - you need increasing amounts of it to get high or if you're suffering from any serious health, psychological, relationship, social, school, work, legal or financial problems because of booze and you continue to drink in spite of these problems, you're an alcoholic. And a moderate drinking approach won't work for you.

Make Your Commitment to Change

Vowing to make a change for the better is the cornerstone of your healthy new drinking foundation. Right here, right now, resolve to proactively work and complete the program so you can achieve your goals of improved drinking habits and reduced alcohol consumption. No excuses!

Take five minutes and write down your commitment to moderate drinking and applying the sensible drinking skills and strategies you'll learn to your everyday life. Reflect on your commitment every day. And remind yourself of it especially when the going gets tough.

Always keep your moderate drinking commitment in the back of your mind. It will see you through the ups and downs of behavior change!

Own the Drink/Link Change Your Drinking Behavior Formula

How do you actually change your problem drinking habits? With the Drink/Link Change Your Drinking Behavior Formula: equal parts of motivation, moderate drinking tools and concepts and positive rein-forcement. Motivating yourself to stay on track, putting the safe-drinking techniques to work for you and rewarding yourself for your successes will transform you from a heavy drinker to a light drinker. And you're guaranteed reduced alcohol intake if you apply this formula to your behavior and your life!

If you're ever unsure about how to change or you feel you're not as successful as you should be at cutting down, just refer to this formula for a little guidance. Maybe you're short on motivation. Maybe you're not applying the sensible drinking skills and strategies to your everyday life. Or maybe you're not giving yourself enough credit for your accom-plishments. It's important to note if you're lacking in any one of these areas, you probably won't be able to make the switch to moderate drinking permanently.

No, you don't have to be a genius to improve your drinking habits. You just have to apply the Drink/Link Change Your Drinking Behavior Formula to your thinking, actions and life. If you do, reasonable, prob-lem-free drinking won't be far behind.

Next, Set Your Drink Limits

When you set realistic daily and weekly drink limits in advance, you'll never have to second guess yourself about how much alcohol is right for you. You'll already know - with concrete numbers in place!

Establishing drink limits increases your odds of drinking responsi-bly. But not having limits and leaving your drinking to chance is often a recipe for disaster. You start drinking, the booze takes over, you don't know when to stop and you keep on guzzling. Trouble!

Sticking to one cocktail on drinking days would certainly eliminate a lot of alcohol-related health risks for you. And you'd be adhering to the moderate drinking limit for women set by the Dietary Guidelines for Americans. This should be your ultimate goal.

But in the meantime, if you do decide to go for a higher limit you'd be wise to think in terms of a drink range. For example, a one to two drink limit or a two to three drink limit. If you don't box yourself into one specific number, you give yourself more leeway and you're able to adjust your consumption to your mood and the occasion. You have more flexibility. A realistic drink range might also eliminate the rebelliousness some people feel when they're restricted to a certain number.

Some days it might not be appropriate to drink your maximum limit. You're too busy and you have other things on your mind, so wine just doesn't fit in. On other days, however, when you're relaxing or socializing you may hit your top number. Staying at or under your limit may vary from day to day - depending on your activities.

Setting a drink limit of more than three drinks on drinking days is not a good idea. More than three drinks is too much alcohol and can cause problems. You could develop health problems. Your judgment and coordination become impaired with too much liquor. You might form a drinking habit and become dependent on booze. And you'd be increasing your tolerance to alcohol, so you'd need more of it to enjoy yourself. Best to err on the side of caution when setting your drink limit. The lower, the better.

Setting a weekly drink limit of no more than thirteen drinks would also be wise. Research shows that if you stay within this drink limit, the less likely you'll have alcohol-related problems. But don't feel obligated to max out at thirteen drinks every week. That's not the point of a moderate drinking program! The point is for you to have one or two pops, enjoy yourself and know when to stop. Sometimes, thirteen drinks in one week are way too much - you've got too much going on.

Some people should not drink at all. Anyone under twenty-one, anyone who cannot restrict their drinking to moderate levels, anyone who is thinking of becoming pregnant or is pregnant, anyone who plans to drive, operate machinery or take part in activities that require attention, skill or coordination, anyone taking prescription or over-the-counter medications that may interact with or intensify the effects of alcohol or anyone who has health, psychological, relationship, social, school, work, legal or financial problems that are caused or aggravated by alcohol should not drink period.

What's your realistic drink limit on drinking days? What's your weekly drink limit? Record them.

Always Keep the Drink/Link Basics in Mind

Here are five safe-drinking guidelines borrowed from the Drink/Link Moderate Drinking Program that will make it easier for you to stay within your drink limits. In fact, if you always observed these commonsense tips, you'd never worry about your drinking again! You'd drink moderately all the time - instinctively.

Memorize the Drink/Link Basics. They're designed for you to have fun, but not get so high you're incapable of stopping. Controlling your drinking just got a little easier - with these simple guidelines in place!

Drink/Link Basic One - One Drink Per Hour

Pacing your drinking offers you the pleasure of a cocktail and the luxury of control. You probably drink too fast right now - many people down that first glass in ten or fifteen minutes. That's too quick and can cause problems.

If you slow down and nurse one drink for one hour, however, you'd have sensible drinking made because it takes most of us one hour to metabolize the alcohol in one drink. Think of it. You'd burn off the booze in one toddy by the time you're ready for another. And you wouldn't be getting ahead of yourself - you'd still be capable of stopping when you hit your limit. No worries!

If you think pacing a drink for an hour is impossible, build up to it over time. If it's currently taking you fifteen or twenty minutes to polish off that pop, add an extra five minutes to your drinking time for each drink every week. The next week, you should be up to twenty or twenty-five minutes for a drink and the week after that you should be up to twenty-five or thirty minutes. Get the idea? It's a pretty simple self-control exercise and eventually you should be able to observe the one drink per hour basic.

From now on, every time you pour yourself a cocktail, look at the clock and calculate the time it will take for that glass. Then pace yourself. If you stay within your time limit, congratulations! You've mastered an important moderate drinking skill. But if you finish that cooler before your time is up, wait and don't have another until you've met your time limit. You'll observe the one drink per hour basic one way or another!

Slowing down your drinking is not brain surgery - but it is crucial to controlling it.

Drink/Link Basic Two - Measure Your Drink Portions

You're not only drinking too fast, you're also probably allowing yourself more than one drink at a time. If you pour as much as you like, you never pay attention to how much alcohol is in one drink or you consider a tumbler of vodka to be one cocktail, you have to clean up your act. You no longer have a free pass to decant recklessly.

One drink is one and a half ounces of spirits or hard liquor, like vodka or scotch, five ounces of wine or twelve ounces of beer. If you're a liquor drinker, use a shot glass or measure out one and a half ounces of water and see where it comes in your favorite glass. Take note. You should not exceed this amount from now on. Same goes for wine. Pour five ounces of water into your wine glass, see where it falls and don't go over this amount. And most beers come in twelve ounce bottles, so one bottle is one drink.

Another simple guideline that will keep your alcohol awareness up and your drinking down!

Drink/Link Basic Three - Three Drinking Hours on Drinking Days

Three hours of drinking? That's more than enough time to play. And drinking longer than that is a waste of your precious time. Some days you shouldn't drink at all. It's just not appropriate or you're too busy. If you're running all day and taking care of business, trying to squeeze in three hours of drinking just doesn't make sense.

On days you do drink, look at the clock, figure out how long three hours is and enjoy yourself without going over your time limit. Of course, three hours is your maximum drinking time. Limiting your drinking to an hour or two would be even better. The shorter your drinking time, the less you'll drink!

Drink/Link Basic Four - Eat Before and During Drinking

Eating before and during drinking is a cardinal moderate drinking rule! Having something in your stomach when you imbibe protects your delicate stomach lining, the liquor doesn't get into your bloodstream as fast as it does on an empty stomach, you don't become impaired as quickly and you're still capable of maintaining control and staying within your drink limits. So many great reasons to eat while you drink, so little time!

You don't have to gorge yourself or eat fattening foods. Healthy snacks, like a handful of nuts or cheese and whole grain crackers, would do the trick without putting the pounds on. From now on, you're eating before and during drinking.

And if you think you'll put on weight if you eat and drink, think again. When you drink on an empty stomach, you're more likely to lose control and over drink - consuming lots of extra alcohol calories actually causing you to gain weight. Just another terrific argument for eating while drinking!

Drink/Link Basic Five - Plan on Two or More Alcohol-Free Days A Week

Taking a break from booze a couple of days a week will make you less dependent on it - physically and psychologically - and help you to put it in perspective. Besides, you'll feel great about yourself for abstaining - especially if you're chained to an everyday drinking habit. It's just another valuable exercise that will increase your self-control around spirits.

If you haven't had an alcohol-free day for a while and feel a little nervous about it, relax. It's not as hard as you think and here are five pointers to help you breeze through it. First, try to abstain on days when you're too busy to kick back with a cocktail. Second, make sure you've got lots of tasty non-alcoholic beverages on hand and drink them instead. Third, if you do have time on your hands on your designated alcohol-free days, make sure you've planned plenty of distracting activities to fill in your old drinking times. And follow through with those activities! Fourth, if you do experience an intense desire to drink, simply wait it out. Psychologists say it only takes five or ten minutes to forget about a craving, so hang in there, have a soft drink and do something to take your mind off of the urge. The craving will pass. And fifth, remind yourself that you talk yourself into and out of things all day long. And you can talk yourself out of drinking too - by reflecting on all of your very important reasons for wanting to reduce your alcohol consumption. Practice these five suggestions when you're taking a break from booze and you'll make an alcohol-free day happen - painlessly.

Interrupt your drinking pattern and you'll not only decrease your drinking desire, you'll decrease your drinking too!

Now, Learn to Motivate Yourself to Stay on Track

How do you motivate yourself to stay within your drink limits and apply the moderate drinking tools you'll learn to your drinking and your life? You'll constantly remind yourself of all of the excellent reasons behind your decision to cut down and control your drinking. And you'll envision how much better your life will be if you drank less. Learning how to motivate yourself to stick to the program is an important component of the Drink/Link Change Your Drinking Behavior Formula. Learn it!

For starters, you'll feel great in the morning. No more agonizing hangovers or feeling dazed and confused after a night of serious partying. You'll feel energetic and positive, not tired, slow and moody. You won't worry about blacking out. You'll remember everything. Just imagine waking up every morning feeling fresh, fit and clear-headed when you drink less. . .

You won't worry about alcohol-related health problems either. Developing liver disease, pancreatitis, heart disease or breast cancer because of drinking would rarely cross your mind. Or checking out early because of alcohol abuse. You'll no longer obsess about your growing dependence on liquor. Or that you might become an alcoholic. If alcoholism runs in your family, you know you don't want to go there. Just imagine the robust health and peace of mind you'll enjoy when you drink less . . .

And think about how good you'll feel about yourself - if you cut down. Your self-esteem and self-confidence will soar. You'll enjoy the self-respect and self-assurance you need to shoot for and achieve your personal, professional and financial goals - without booze and its problems holding you back. You'll love yourself for always maintaining control. You'll have tons of time and energy for family and friends. And you'll leave all of the shame, embarrassment and guilt you feel about your heavy drinking behind. No more beating yourself up over alcohol - psychological hangovers. Instead, you'll feel fabulous - worthy, successful, a good person. Imagine feeling great about yourself - confident, strong and capable - when you drink less . . .

You could restore your precious reputation too. What people think of you as a woman, wife, mother, friend, professional and valued member of the community. Your reputation is so important to you and so hard to get back once it's been tainted by alcohol abuse. You'll be seen as a better partner and friend. You'll be known as a great mother and role model to your kids. You'll be an appreciated employee and colleague. Imagine recovering your sterling reputation and people thinking highly of you when you drink less . . .

Drinking will no longer come between you and your family and friends. You'll no longer alienate those close to you because you drink too much. You'll never be afraid of what you might say or do around your loved ones when you're drinking. You'll never again engage in out-of-control behavior. You might be happier with your partner and kids - if wine was no longer an issue. Less alcohol will translate into improved relationships. Imagine how much better your relationships might be when you drink less . . .

Alcohol-related work, financial and legal problems would also be eliminated if you cut down. No more being late or hung over at work. You'll be sharper, do a better job and be more productive. You might even get a raise or promotion because you're so good at what you do - if problem drinking was no longer an issue. And no more worries about getting a DUI or DWI or having child custody complications because of your hard drinking. Imagine never having to deal with alcohol-related work, financial or legal problems when you drink less . . .

Now, record all of your very good reasons supporting your decision to drink sensibly. Then write down all the areas of your life that will improve when you follow through with your moderate drinking commitment. Keep your reasons and your vision of a healthier, happier life on hand at all times - in your wallet, purse, coat pocket, on your laptop or phone - so you can refer to them at any time.

These reasons and your vision of a better life make up your motivational pep talk - self-talk meant to deter bad drinking habits and encourage good ones. Make a point of taking ten minutes everyday and giving yourself a passionate motivational pep talk - reflecting on why you want to drink less and the positive changes you'll enjoy if you do. Give yourself a pep talk before any and every drinking occasion too. Your pep talk will motivate you to apply the healthy drinking skills and concepts you'll learn to your behavior and your life - enabling you to stick to your drink limits.

Just like the Drink/Link Basics, your motivational pep talk is yours for life and will serve you well - if you use it. It will get you excited about moderate drinking and keep you on track!

Reward Yourself When You Succeed

Giving yourself a pat on the back for a job well done is another crucial component of the Drink/Link Change Your Drinking Behavior Formula. If you reward yourself when you play by the moderate drinking rules, you'll be reinforcing your safe new drinking habits. And soon, they'll feel natural to you and become deeply ingrained. Payoff! So every time you stick to your drink limits and avoid going overboard - especially when you're tempted to - recognize your accomplishment and treat yourself.

Your reward may be something as simple as saying to yourself, "I'm amazing. I just passed up a third glass of wine! I'm fabulous". Or "I ate and didn't drink on an empty stomach! I'm the best". Telling yourself you're the greatest when you stick to your limit or follow through with a moderate drinking skill or make the best of a risky drinking situation may be all you need to own your healthy new drinking habits for life.

Or maybe you'd like a more tangible treat. A new outfit? A day at the spa? A hot fudge sundae? Dinner out? A trip to Hawaii? A gold bracelet? Spoil yourself with something special for all the times you say no to that extra drink. Savor your successes! A concrete prize is also a good way to say "great job" to yourself.

Take time right now and record a list of rewards and positive statements you can say to yourself when you stick to the program and drink moderately. Light drinking will get easier and easier - if you treat yourself every time you do something right!

Start Your Drinking Diary Too

Research shows you'll automatically reduce your alcohol consumption when you monitor your drinking. You'll not only drink less, you'll also become sensitive to the internal and external cues that trigger your drinking too. So keeping a drinking diary is a good thing in more ways than one.

From now on, during or soon after every drinking party, record the number of drinks you had, how long you drank, the day and time of day you drank, what the occasion was, who your drinking companions were, the location of the drinking party, your mood and physical state and if you stuck to your limit or went overboard.

Tuning in to your drinking cues is a big deal because once you're aware of them, you'll be less susceptible to them and you'll no longer engage in mindless drinking. External drinking cues are the most obvious ones to spot. They're the people, places and circumstances that trip your desire to drink. Internal ones, on the other hand, are a little harder to put your finger on. They're physiological sensations or psychological states. Hunger, fatigue, pain, emotions, moods and mental health conditions are all internal cues that may press your buttons.

Recording how much you're drinking and the specifics of the drinking party is your mission from now on. Store this information on your laptop, phone or dig up a notebook and write it down. If you're faithful to your diary, you'll not only get smarter about your drinking, you'll drink less too. Keep it forever or until you get so good at moderating you no longer need it.

Your Goal is to Stay Under a .06 BAC

Wonderful things happen when you're thoughtful about your drinking and you stay under a .06 BAC. You can have fun, but you're still in control and can slow down or stop when the time comes. You'll lower your tolerance to alcohol too. In fact, if you stick to your drink limits and stay under a .06 BAC every time you drink, within two weeks you'll have a lower tolerance for liquor and you won't need as much of it to get high. Payoff!

Refer to the Blood Alcohol Concentration Charts in Chapter One. How many drinks can you have within one, two and three hours and still stay under a .06 BAC? Write these numbers down and always keep them in mind. Make good on keeping your BAC down and you'll make good on keeping your drinking down.

Replace a Bad Habit with a Good One

It only takes three weeks, twenty-one short days, for you to improve your drinking behavior. All you have to do is diligently work the program and do everything that's asked of you and you'll be drinking less within weeks.

Hang in there! You can change the course of your drinking and your life - in practically no time. Remember that for the next three weeks. It might keep you on track so you can reach your ultimate goal - a take it or leave it attitude about drinking and alcohol forever.

Consider An Alcohol-Free Period

You'd be wise to give yourself a time out from spirits before you throw yourself wholeheartedly into moderate drinking. There are several advantages to an abstinent period prior to starting the program. If you're a habitual drinker, it will get you out of your old drinking rut. It will also take the focus off of alcohol for a while which will improve your chances of cutting down. Finally, it will minimize the role of liquor in your life - making it easier for you to follow through with your healthy new drinking ways.

One week? Two weeks? A month? Six months? A breather from booze will make your moderate drinking transition less difficult. Think about it . . .

Lay Your Moderate Drinking Foundation

Define Moderate Drinking

Make Your Commitment to Change

Own the Drink/Link Change Your Drinking Behavior Formula

Set Your Drink Limits

Always Keep the Drink/Link Basics in Mind

Learn to Motivate Yourself to Stay on Track

Reward Yourself When You Succeed

Start Your Drinking Diary

Your Goal is to Stay Under a .06 BAC

Replace a Bad Habit with a Good One

Consider an Alcohol-Free Period Before You Start the Program

∞ *Chapter 6* ∞

Seventeen Terrific Tips to Painlessly Stay Within Your Drink Limits

Y ou've laid a solid moderate drinking foundation, now you're going to frame your healthy new habits with simple skills and concepts to observe the Drink/Link Basics and stay within your drink limits. These tips may seem simple, but don't let that fool you. They really work if you apply them to your drinking and your life.

With these suggestions, you'll not only have fun with a cocktail or two - without losing it, you'll also grow greater self-control and self-confidence around alcohol. And once you get them down, you'll feel certain you can tackle bigger challenges ahead.

1. Always Preplan Your Drinking

Knowing how much you'll drink and how long you'll drink - before that glass even touches your lips - might be the most valuable strategy you'll ever learn to control your drinking. You won't be leaving your drinking to chance and you'll be less likely to overdo it - if you preplan how much and how long you'll drink.

Keep your drink limit and the Drink/Link Basics in mind when planning for a drinking event. How many drinks will you have? How long will you drink? How long will you nurse each drink? What will you eat before and during drinking?

If you've set a one to two daily drink limit, you can have one or two pops. Two hours is plenty of time to enjoy yourself, even though the basics allow you up to three drinking hours. You'll look at the clock and pace each drink for as long as possible - with one hour being your ultimate goal. You'll also have a wholesome snack before you start drinking and continue to eat while you're drinking. Between your drink limit and the basics, you'll take the guesswork out of your drinking - and make responsible drinking happen.

Below, there are many more helpful tips you can insert into your drinking plans - making staying within your drink limits easier than you imagined. Preparing a plan for every drinking occasion will keep you in line and out of trouble. Do it!

2. Clean Up Your Sloppy Drinking Habits

Over the years, you've probably picked up some pretty sloppy drinking habits. Most of us have. You've gotten careless about how you drink and your alcohol consumption reflects it. Now it's time for you to pay closer attention to your poor drinking form and polish it up. Your payoffs for cleaning up your act? More control and less liquor!

One of the biggest obstacles to slowing down your drinking might be that you're gulping that pop instead of sipping it. Over time, you've become accustomed to the flavor of your favorite toddy so you swill it down without even thinking. You imbibe mindlessly. From now on, remind yourself to sip, don't gulp. What's your hurry? You'll still have fun.

Another obstacle to you pacing your drinking might be that you're keeping that glass in your hand at all times. Hanging on to that cocktail just reminds you that you've got alcohol to drink. And it's way too easy to guzzle when you've always got a grip on it. From now on, put your drink down between sips.

Also, give yourself a five minute break between swallows. You don't have to have one sip after another until that brew is gone. No, take your time, set your drink down between sips and relax. Have a taste every five minutes and you'll stretch your drink.

Practice proper drinking etiquette and you'll be practicing moderate drinking. Insert these suggestions into your basic drinking plans to help you stay within your drink limits.

3. Delay Your Drinking

Do you really have to have a cooler right out of the gate when you're partying? Do you rush to pour yourself a pop when the clock strikes five? Is that glass of wine a must immediately when you come home from work? Can't wait to have a cocktail as soon as you hit your favorite watering hole? When the kids are in bed, do you make a beeline for the vodka? When you get together with the girls, is a margarita the first item on your agenda? When the play date starts, does your drinking start too?

Break these patterns now. When you find yourself slipping into your old drinking routine, look at the clock, wait ten or fifteen minutes and do something different. Have a soft drink. Make some popcorn. Get involved in conversation. Connect with your friends, partner or kids. Water the plants. Start dinner. Call a friend. After you've delayed for at least ten or fifteen minutes, then pour yourself a cocktail. Do the same when you're thinking about having a second or third glass too.

Delaying your first drink and successive drinks helps you to pace your drinking, you down less liquor and you're making a powerful statement to yourself: you control alcohol, alcohol does not control you. Insert these suggestions into your basic drinking plans to help you stay within your drink limits.

4. Alternate with Non-Alcoholic Drinks

No, your world does not revolve around alcohol. Or at least it shouldn't. That's why you should start alternating with non-alcoholic drinks. So instead of automatically having another margarita, have seltzer water with a squeeze of lime or a glass of lemonade. You'll feel good about yourself for having so much self-control and you'll be slowing down too - but you'll still be enjoying yourself.

What's your favorite soft drink? If you're not sure, take a stroll down the beverage aisle of your favorite supermarket or department store.

There's a huge selection of exciting non-alcoholic refreshments on the market these days and there must be one or two that will strike your fancy. Who needs one cocktail after another? Not you.

Stock up on your favorite soft drinks today. That way you'll never have an excuse to avoid alternating. And start talking yourself into the notion that you can be satisfied with a non-alcoholic beverage. You might just start believing it! Insert these suggestions into your basic drinking plans to help you stay within your drink limits.

5. Lighten Up

If you love shots or strong mixed drinks, it's time to rethink your drinking choices. Hard liquor packs a wallop - a lot of alcohol into a small drink - so maybe you'd be better off with something a little taller and a little tamer.

With a shot, you're done in one sip. With a potent mixed drink - like a martini - you're done in three or four sips. And you reach your drink limit before you know it. But if you switched to beer or wine, which are larger, healthier alternatives, you'd have more to drink and you'd be able to nurse that drink longer because there's more of it. Make sense?

You'll not only be stretching your drinking time because you have a larger pop, you'll also be slowing down because you're not use to the taste of it. When you're not familiar with a drink, you're not into it like your old favorite - making it easier for you to pace yourself.

You're still having a cocktail, it's just a different cocktail. You're just opting out of the strong stuff for something a little lighter and larger. Insert this suggestion into your basic drinking plans to help you stay within your drink limits.

6. Distract Yourself from Drinking

Taking your mind off of that first drink and successive drinks with distracting activities is another brilliant strategy to nurse liquor. You'll get a lot done and, who knows, you might even forget about that vodka tonic altogether!

Sit down and record a list of twenty distracting activities you can kick into whenever you're thinking about having a stiff one. Simple things -

MODERATE DRINKING MY WAY

like taking a walk, tending your garden or having a snack. Or more complicated things - like going to a yoga class or doing a crossword puzzle. Or fun things - like seeing a matinee, window shopping or taking a dance class. Be sure to include things you can do at home too, especially if most of your drinking happens at home - like giving yourself a manicure or pedicure, soaking in a bubble bath, taking a nap, watching puppies or kitties on the Animal Planet or playing a game of solitaire.

The next time you're obsessing about having a cooler, stop and refer to your list of distracting activities. Then tackle one. Take your mind off of drinking and drinking less will follow! Insert this suggestion into your basic drinking plans to help you stay within your drink limits.

7. Focus on People, Conversation and Activities - Not Alcohol

Do you get a little nervous when your glass is half empty? Do you order another drink even though there's a little left in the one you already have? Do you have to order another cocktail immediately after you've finished one? If you do any of these things, you're a little too attached to booze and it's time to detach.

Instead of focusing on that drink, turn on to the people, conversation, activities and surroundings of the drinking party. Strike up a conversation with your partner, family or friends. Or put your heart and soul into whipping up a gourmet meal if you're at home. Or network and make new friends if you're at a social event. Dance. Play games. Tell jokes. Play the piano. Notice the architectural details of that great new restaurant. Whatever. Pour yourself into the people, conversation, activities and surroundings of the event, instead of pouring yourself another glass of wine.

Alcohol is a mere complement to your life. It's not the main event. Make this mental shift and you'll not only be minimizing its importance in your life, you'll be minimizing your drinking too. Insert these suggestions into your basic drinking plans to help you stay within your drink limits.

8. Consider Your Feelings Before You Drink

Don't expose yourself to a drinking party when you're hungry or tired. Don't challenge yourself with a bash when you're in a bad mood. When you're not quite one hundred percent - physically or psychologically - you're setting yourself up for a drinking mistake.

Consider imbibing only when you're up to it. You'll increase your chances of sticking to your drinking plan and drink limits if you do. Simply put, the better you feel, the less likely you'll blow it. Insert these suggestions into your basic drinking plans to help you stay within your drink limits.

9. Rethink Heavy Drinking Occasions

You don't have to attend every drinking party you're invited to. If you know it's going to be a free-for-all, it certainly increases your odds of getting smashed. And you don't have to dance until the break of dawn if you do go. The later you stay, the longer you might drink and the more likely you'll lose it.

Evaluate risky events ahead of time and determine if it would be in your best interest to attend them in the first place or if you should limit your time at them if you do go. It will be easier for you to stay within your drink limits if you do.

From now on, before you hit a big bash you should consciously decide if you should even go or if you should leave early. You take charge of drinking occasions, they don't take charge of you! Insert these suggestions into your basic drinking plans to help you stay within your drink limits.

10. Get Comfortable Saying No to Alcohol

If you're going to succeed at moderate drinking, you're going to have to say "no" - verbally or non-verbally - to alcohol at times. It's unavoidable. You'll have to go out of your way to make it known that you're not interested in drinking. Period.

A couple of secrets to saying no to booze without ruffling anyone's feathers? Try to be cool, casual and to the point. And if that doesn't work, give your host a good excuse. An honest one would be nice, like you're driving or you have to get home to the kids. But if that doesn't work, make something up, like you've got a big day at work tomorrow or you're running a marathon in the morning. Whatever works.

Another secret to passing on alcohol? Getting the polite refusal down. When you have a quiet moment, imagine situations in which you'd say no to a cocktail. And imagine the polite refusals you'd use to avoid drinking. Then rehearse them out loud or silently to yourself, so when the time comes and you need them you'll feel comfortable saying no.

Here are some polite refusals you should practice and have on hand whenever you drink:

- "No, thanks."
- "I'm fine right now."
- "I'm taking a break."
- "I've had enough."
- "I'm not drinking tonight."
- "I don't drink."
- "Can I have a soda instead?"
- "I'm tired and another drink would put me to sleep."
- "I'm done drinking and I'm going home."
- "I have a big day tomorrow."
- "I don't want to have a hangover tomorrow."
- "I don't drink and drive."
- "I'm high enough."

Once you've perfected the polite refusal and have said no to spirits a couple of times, it will be easier for you to refuse it in the future. Insert these suggestions into your basic drinking plans to help you stay within your drink limits.

11. Know When You're Caught Up in the Moment

Maybe you lose it in social situations. You're talking, laughing, drinking and having a grand old time and you're not really thinking about controlling your drinking or pacing yourself, so you're getting pretty high. A dicey situation for someone committed to moderate drinking. If only you could catch yourself, remind yourself you're under the influence and that alcohol could get the best of you if you're not careful.

Maybe then you'd come back to your senses and try to stay within your drink limits.

The next time you're partying and wine and commonsense are running away with you, give yourself a reality check. Every fifteen minutes assess how high you are and ask yourself if it's time to slow down or stop drinking. Maybe that will bring you back to reality and you'll refocus on your limits.

When you're drinking and you know you're getting caught up in the moment, that's your cue to get back in the moderate drinking game and start managing your drinking. Insert these suggestions into your basic drinking plans to help you stay within your drink limits.

12. Compromise When the Going Gets Tough

When you feel torn - when you really want another drink, but you've reached your limit and you know you shouldn't continue drinking - try compromising with yourself. Perhaps allowing yourself just a few more sips might satisfy that need and you'd be okay with stopping at that point.

Unfortunately, some people think if they exceed their limit by just a little they've failed and since they've already blown it, they might as well get drunk. They throw the baby out with the bathwater.

Stop thinking this way. No, if you really want another cocktail compromise with yourself and have just one or two more sips. Hopefully, that will be the end of it. And if you still want to carry on, allow yourself just one more drink. But after that, you're done compromising. And you're finished drinking.

Black and white, all-or-nothing-at-all thinking won't get you to a moderate drinking place, but flexible, compromising thinking will. Insert these suggestions into your basic drinking plans to help you stay within your drink limits.

13. Think Before Reacting and Drinking

If drinking is a kneejerk reaction for you at times and you automatically guzzle when you're with certain people or in certain situations, stop and think instead. If you pause and reflect on what you're doing and the reactive nature of your behavior, you can change it and your problem drinking pattern.

So the next time you catch yourself drinking without thinking, take a break and a step back. Then do something different, like having a soft drink, engaging in conversation or giving yourself a motivational pep talk. You'll put an end to your reflexive drinking if you do.

You can change your old drinking ways with a little reflection and a good replacement activity. Insert these suggestions into your basic drinking plans to help you stay within your drink limits.

14. A Little Control is Better Than None

Sometimes, you may not be in the mood to control your drinking. You're ready to throw in the towel and drink like you did in the bad old days - before you made your moderate drinking commitment. The program and your impulse control are out the window and you could care less.

Wait a minute. Don't toss them out quite yet. You don't have to totally revert back to your old problem drinking behavior and get blotto when your impulses are getting the best of you. No, when you're in one of these moods, chill. And practice just a few of the sensible drinking skills you've learned. A little restraint might prevent you from really blowing it and feeling awful the next day.

A little impulse control is better than no control at all. Think about that the next time you're in one of those moods. Insert these suggestions into your basic drinking plans to help you stay within your drink limits.

15. Three Questions to Decide If You Should Stop Drinking

Am I high enough? Have I reached my limit? Do I really want another drink? Here are three questions you should ask yourself when you're under the influence and you're not quite sure if you should quit or have another drink. They're an objective solution to your subjective dilemma and they'll take the guesswork out of your drinking decision!

If you answer yes to the first two questions, you're done. If you answer no to the first two questions and yes to the last one, you can have another cocktail. It's that simple. Who said knowing when to stop drinking was hard?

And you don't have to wait until you're thinking about stopping to make good use of these questions. Ask them before any drink, any time. You might be surprised at how often you feel satisfied and you're ready to quit - before you even hit your limit.

You'll raise your alcohol awareness, eliminate mindless drinking and reduce your alcohol consumption if you check in with these questions before every pop. Payoffs galore! Insert these suggestions into your basic drinking plans to help you stay within your drink limits.

16. Devise a Stop Drinking Plan

You've learned to make a drinking plan for every drinking occasion. Now it's imperative for you to devise a stop drinking plan for when you've hit your drink limit. So instead of feeling deprived and ob-sessing about having another cocktail, you'll swing into your stop drinking plan - what you'll do and say to yourself to avoid more drinking comfortably.

Start with a passionate motivational pep talk. That should get you out of the drinking mood. Remember all of your very important reasons for wanting to cut down? Remember what your healthy new life will look like when you drink less? Daydreaming about all of the benefits of reducing your alcohol consumption might be all you need to stop drinking easily.

Make sure you've planned distracting activities to take your mind off of another glass too. If you can distract yourself with another activity, you'll probably forget all about that margarita in five or ten minutes. Turn on the TV, have a snack, check your email or brush your teeth and soon continued drinking will be the furthest thing from your mind. List ten distracting activities that will deter you from continued drinking when it's time to quit. Then engage in one when you need to!

When you make a stop drinking plan beforehand, you can quit drinking the easy way - not the hard way. The easy way is to know what you'll do and say to yourself when it's time to stop. The hard way is to not have a plan and to long for another forbidden cocktail. Insert these suggestions into your basic drinking plans to help you stay within your drink limits.

17. Now Put These Tips to Work for You . . .

Look at your coming week. When will you be drinking? How many drinks will you have, how long will you drink and what strategies and techniques will you put into play to stay within your drink limits for each potential drinking party? Take pen to paper this very minute and jot down a drinking plan for every drinking occasion you anticipate. Then refresh your memory and go over them before each event. Finally, follow through with them when the time comes!

A well-thought-out plan before every drinking occasion might be the secret of your moderate drinking success. Put it into action!

Seventeen Terrific Tips to Painlessly Stay Within Your Dink Limits

1. Always Preplan Your Drinking Behavior
2. Clean Up Your Sloppy Drinking Habits
3. Delay Your Drinking
4. Alternate with Non-Alcoholic Drinks
5. Lighten Up
6. Distract Yourself from Drinking
7. Focus on People, Conversation, Activities and Surroundings
8. Consider Your Feelings Before You Drink
9. Rethink Heavy Drinking Occasions
10. Get Comfortable Saying No to Alcohol
11. Know When You're Caught Up in the Moment
12. Compromise When the Going Gets Tough
13. Think Before Reacting and Drinking
14. A Little Control is Better Than None
15. Three Questions to Decide if You Should Stop Drinking
16. Devise a Stop Drinking Plan
17. Put These Tips to Work for You . . .

Chapter 7

Control Your Drinking Triggers, Cycle and Thinking

Have you been keeping your drinking diary? Are you becoming familiar with the triggers that start you drinking and keep you drinking? Good. Now you'll explore ways to handle these cues in healthy ways so they don't lead to overdrinking.

You'll also investigate your drinking cycle and drinking thinking. Understanding how your cycle works and tuning into your self-talk that rationalizes your drinking will not only raise your alcohol awareness, but lower your consumption too.

Take at least one week to absorb all the information in this chapter and apply everything you learn to your thinking and behavior. When you control your drinking triggers, cycle and thinking, you'll control your drinking!

External Drinking Cues

Drinking places, companions and circumstances might be external drinking cues for you - increasing your desire to drink and resulting in problem drinking. If most of your heavy drinking happens at your home, a friend's house, a favorite restaurant or hangout, these places are drinking triggers for you. You associate alcohol with the environment, give yourself permission to imbibe and may even get wasted.

Drinking companions may also press your buttons. If you always drink or overdo it in the company of a certain person or group of people, these individuals are drinking triggers for you. Drinking is expected when you're with them and getting loaded is no big deal.

Drinking circumstances, like parties, play dates, girl's night out, book club gatherings, vacations, weddings, holidays and celebrations, may lead you to drink too. You always tipple when you're involved in these activities and sometimes you overindulge.

Or perhaps just the sight, sound or smell of booze stimulates your alcohol appetite. Just seeing the margaritas being poured or hearing the clink of glasses gets you going and you drink too much.

Look over your drinking diary. What external drinking cues trigger your drinking? People? Places? Circumstances? The sight, sound or smell of liquor? List them.

Internal Drinking Cues

Physiological sensations, like hunger, thirst, pain and fatigue, might be internal drinking cues for you - sparking your desire to drink and causing heavy drinking. If you're hungry, you drink wine. If you're thirsty, you drink beer. If you're aching, you swill vodka. Or if you're tired, you down a martini.

Feelings and moods may also be internal drinking cues for you. You might drink to feel even better, if you're happy. You might drink to lift your spirits, if you're in the dumps. You might drink to take the edge off of loneliness or boredom. You might drink to cope with depression or stress. Or you might drink to fill a void in your life.

Look over your drinking diary. What internal drinking cues drive you to drink? Physiological sensations, like hunger, thirst, pain or fatigue? Negative feelings like sadness, anger, frustration, boredom, loneliness, stress or depression? Positive feelings like happiness, excitement, satisfaction or peace of mind? Or both positive and negative feelings? List them.

How to Handle Drinking Cues So They Don't Drive You to Drink

Before you were aware of your drinking cues, they were probably having their way with you. You mindlessly caved into them and drank. Now take back your power and control your drinking triggers, so they don't control you. And here are five simple strategies to help you do just that.

One of the easiest ways to defuse a nagging drinking cue is to simply deal with it appropriately. That is, if you're famished, eat, if you're parched, have a non-alcoholic beverage, if you're in pain, take a pain reliever or see your doctor or if you're tired, rest. This is not rocket science.

A second way to neutralize a cue that leads to problem drinking is to eliminate it. Avoid the risky people, places and circumstances that encourage your drinking and you'll avoid the overdrinking that happens when you're exposed to them. If that means you no longer associate with hard drinkers who are a bad influence on you, you no longer frequent establishments where you go all out and get smashed or you no longer get yourself into circumstances where you lose control, so be it. It may be hard at first, but it will be worth your while in the long run. You'll stop falling into your old problem drinking trap - if you avoid the people, places and circumstances that have supported your unhealthy drinking.

Another option to managing a trigger is to limit your exposure to it. Before you get together with binge drinking pals, before you hit your favorite club or before you go to that wild party, set a time limit and keep it. Instead of drinking the night away, limit yourself to one, two or three hours with dicey people, at dangerous places or in hazardous situations. Stick to a time limit and you'll be more likely to stick to your drink limit.

A fourth possibility to controlling a drinking cue is to weaken it. When you're bored and lonely and hankering for a cocktail, call a friend or get busy with an entertaining activity - instead of hitting the bottle. When you're starving around five and dying for a drink, have an appetizer or dinner - instead of pouring yourself a glass of wine. When you're having a fit and want a pop to settle down, process your feelings, talk about them and get them off your chest - instead of using booze to chill. Weaken the trigger and you'll weaken your drinking desire.

Finally, change the way you perceive or think about a drinking cue so it no longer affects you or your alcohol intake. When you look at a trigger from different angles, you put it in a more realistic light. It's really just a person, place, situation, feeling, mood or sensation that shouldn't necessarily lead to drinking. Detach and view your cues objectively - instead of seeing them subjectively and emotionally. When you change your mind about them and put them in perspective, you won't be so susceptible to them.

Now it's your turn. Write a specific plan for each and every drinking cue that fuels your drinking. Some may be canceled out with just one simple strategy. But others might require several different approaches. Control your drinking cues and you'll control your drinking!

Tips to modify your drinking cues . . .

Treat the cue appropriately

Eliminate the cue

Limit your exposure to the cue

Weaken the cue

Change the way you perceive and think about the
cue

What's Your Drinking Cycle?

What happens inside of your head when you're contemplating drinking and you decide to go for it? Most of us experience a fairly predictable drinking cycle that leads to that first drink. And this is probably how your drinking cycle works - in a nutshell.

The first phase of your cycle starts with drinking cues. You're exposed to risky triggers, internal or external or both, that start you thinking about a cocktail.

The second stage of your cycle involves drinking thinking - untrue or illogical thoughts and self-talk that encourage you to drink. Common drinking thinking sounds like, "I've had a tough day today and I need a drink" or "I went to the park with the kids, so I deserve a glass of wine" or "Everyone else is drinking too much, so I'll have another martini too" or "I'd better have a vodka now before the kids get home". Simply put, in your drinking thinking stage you justify your drinking.

In the third phase of your drinking cycle, you give in to your impulses and pour yourself a pop. Initially, you feel relaxed and happy. If you play by the rules, nurse your drink and stay under a .06 BAC, you'll enjoy yourself but you'll still be able to slow down and stop when you hit your drink limit. But if you don't play by the rules, don't nurse your drink and exceed a .06 BAC, you'll become mentally and physically impaired, lose control and might blow your limit.

The fourth stage is decision making time. Should you stop at your limit or continue to drink? If you've behaved yourself, stopping at your limit will be easy. But if you haven't behaved yourself, stopping at your limit will be difficult. The decision is yours.

There you have it. The drinking cycle that most of us experience. Odds are you were never aware of it. But now that you're on to it, you'll no longer be a slave to it.

Stages of your drinking cycle . . .

Drinking cues gather

Drinking thinking encourages you to drink

You drink - reasonably or recklessly

You stop or continue to drink

Derail Your Drinking Cycle

You can interrupt your drinking cycle in any one of the thinking or action stages of it. And if you can disrupt it in any way, you can beat it and problem drinking!

One way to derail your cycle is to address the drinking cues in the first phase. When you see the perfect storm of drinking triggers gathering, deal with each one individually so the tempest doesn't form in the first place. If you're hungry, eat. If you're sad, cry. If you're lonely, you call a friend. Heading off a disaster by managing menacing drinking cues early on is better than second guessing yourself later.

If you're in the drinking thinking phase and you're talking yourself into partying, get a grip. First, look at what you're saying to yourself to rationalize your drinking. Is it appropriate to use alcohol to make up for a bad day? No. Is it logical to have a glass of wine because you took the kids to the park? No. Refute untrue, illogical excuses to drink and you'll deactivate them. Then counter them with rational self-talk. Listening to your favorite music is a therapeutic way to handle a bad day. Soaking in the hot tub is a good way to unwind after a day in the park with the kids. Get the idea?

Replacing negative thoughts that lead you to drink with positive ones that downplay liquor is also a good technique to counteract drinking thinking. When you're craving a cosmopolitan, reflect on your successes - the times you've stayed within your drink limits - instead of wallowing in your overdrinking failures. Think of how wonderful you feel physically and psychologically in the morning when you drink moderately - instead of what a miserable person you are because you're battling the bottle. Stay positive and talk back to negative thinking that trips your drinking desire. Then it will no longer rule your drinking or your life.

Another straightforward strategy to divert your problem drinking cycle is to simply vow to stop drinking once you've hit your limit. Quit no matter what. That will certainly put an end to the cycle. Swearing to stop once you've reached your limit - even though you're under the influence and may want to continue - is a no-brainer that eliminates a lot of self-talk and painful indecision.

Identifying the thinking and action stages of your drinking cycle and modifying them in some way will break your old drinking patterns. Another important tactic to defeat problem drinking!

Derail your drinking cycle . . .

Disrupt your drinking cycle in the thinking or action stages of it

Defuse drinking cues as they arise

Refute illogical self-talk that rationalizes drinking

Replace negative thinking with positive thinking

Stick to your drink limit no matter what

Step Four

Cultivate a Moderate Drinking Mindset and Lifestyle

∞ *Chapter 8* ∞

Start Thinking and Living Like a Moderate Drinker

To enjoy safe drinking forever, you need to acquire a moderate drinking mindset and lifestyle - minimizing the importance of alcohol in your life, putting it in perspective and recognizing that it's just a complement to your life, nothing more. You'll instinctively cut back on booze if you do!

This week, you'll cultivate your moderate drinking mentality and way of life with fifteen fantastic tips to change your mind about drinking and alcohol!

1. Balance is the Key to a Moderate Drinking Mindset and Lifestyle

Living a stable, well-rounded lifestyle will enable you to enjoy controlled drinking forever. If you take good care of yourself and don't go overboard or spread yourself too thin in any one area of your life - physically, psychologically, interpersonally, socially, intellectually, professionally, financially or spiritually - you'll be less inclined to abuse alcohol. A balanced lifestyle breeds harmony and satisfaction and promotes healthy attitudes, habits and drinking.

But an unbalanced lifestyle breeds chaos and dissatisfaction and leads to unhealthy attitudes, habits and drinking. Staring at the computer twenty hours a day and not getting any physical activity or working eighty hours a week and foregoing a social life or partying day and night and not paying your bills or spending all of your time at the gym and ignoring your spiritual side are all examples of lopsided lifestyles which can cause problems - and alcohol abuse.

Live a steady life and you'll enjoy a take it or leave it attitude about spirits!

2. Cozy Up to the Concept of Appropriate Drinking

Appropriate drinking is drinking that's suited to the occasion. It usually involves people, socializing and food - with a few exceptions. And it's never, ever going over your drink limit or getting drunk.

Dinner out with your partner can be an appropriate drinking occasion. Celebrating a special event with a glass of champagne can be an appropriate drinking occasion. Socializing with friends can be an appropriate drinking occasion. And clubbing with pals can be an appropriate drinking occasion. Appropriate drinking involves good times, good food and good people.

Drinking because you're lonely or bored is not appropriate drinking. Drinking to improve your mood is not appropriate drinking. Drinking to pep yourself up is not appropriate drinking, Drinking to feel better about yourself is not appropriate drinking. Drinking for no good reason is not appropriate drinking. Sneaking or hiding drinking is not appropriate drinking. Drinking to fill a void in your life is not appropriate drinking.

From now on, before every cocktail, ask yourself if drinking is suited to the occasion. More often than not, the answer is probably no. That's when you stop, take a step back and think about all of your very good reasons for wanting to cut down - in other words, you give yourself a mini-motivational pep talk. Between a pep talk and switching to a ginger ale, you'll be putting the concept of appropriate drinking to work for you and putting the brakes on problem drinking.

Question your drinking. Question every drink. Then modify your attitude and behavior to fit the situation. You'll be making a meaningful change in your drinking and your life if you do.

3. Cozy Up to the Concept of Mindful Drinking Too

When you sensitize yourself to how much you drink, how you drink and why you drink, you're raising your alcohol awareness. And reactive, reflexive drinking - mindless drinking - will become a thing of the past. You'll evolve into a thoughtful drinker and instead of downing two, three or four glasses of wine without even thinking, you'll take your time, pace yourself and savor your cocktail without getting ahead of yourself.

The beauty of mindful drinking is that you'll not only be nurturing a healthy moderate drinking mindset and lifestyle, you'll also be reducing your alcohol consumption. Mindful drinking equals moderate drinking.

4. Put Alcohol in Perspective

How does liquor fit into your life? Where does it fall on your list of priorities? Does a glass of wine rate high - too high? Does it take precedence over people, activities or obligations? If booze is your top priority, it's time to put it in perspective and remind yourself that it should really just accent your wonderful life, not be the highlight of it. And putting it low on your list of priorities would be a smart move.

Think about how trivial alcohol really is compared to your good health, loved ones, relationships, interests, activities, work, goals and dreams. When you realize how insignificant it should be in your life, you'll be making a major mental shift. And you'll be well on your way to owning a moderate drinking way of life.

Wouldn't it be great if you drank conservatively all the time - without even trying? When you put alcohol in perspective, you'll do just that!

5. Make Alcohol Less Important in Your Life

How important is liquor in your life? More important than your relationship with your partner? More important than being a good parent and role model to your kids? More important than liking yourself and thinking you're a quality person? More important than leading a happy, healthy life?

If alcohol is a little too important to you, how do you eliminate your unhealthy desire for it? One way is to stop yourself when you're thinking about drinking, tell yourself you place too much emphasis on it and you want to make it less important in your life. In other words, you talk yourself out of it.

Another way to minimize wine's importance is to cultivate interests, activities and friendships that don't require it. Strike up relationships with people who aren't into drinking and pursue interests that don't involve spirits. The more alcohol-free socializing and fun you have, the less important booze will become. Put that glass down, get out and party - without beer!

You'll take a step away from alcohol and a step towards a moderate drinking attitude when you talk down drinking and talk up alcohol-free people, entertainment and interests.

6. View Alcohol Realistically

Alcohol is not the be-all or end-all. It's not a friend or a fix. It can't make you happy long-term. It's just alcohol. And you determine its value by how you use it.

If you use it sparingly and control your drinking, it can be an asset. It can be relaxing and stress-reducing. And it can even offer you a few health benefits. But if you drink heavily and don't control it, it becomes a problem - threatening your health, attitude, family, relationships, livelihood and freedom.

Liquor is what it is. When you're realistic about what it can and cannot do for you, the less you'll ask of it and the less you'll drink. And you'll achieve this rational attitude with deep reflection and guided self-talk.

7. Don't Control Your Inner Self with Outside Substances

If you keep your thoughts, emotions and problems bottled up inside of you and you turn to spirits to cope - escaping your troubles temporarily when you're under the influence -rethink your coping style. You're really just trying to fix your inner self with booze, instead of trying to fix your outer problems that are driving you to drink.

Many women tend to bury their troubles and bad feelings. We wait and hope the individuals and situations that are making us unhappy will get better - with a glass in our hand. Unfortunately, we may pay a heavy price for dealing with issues in this way. We might start abusing alcohol or even become addicted to it - when we try to drink our concerns and feelings away.

Forget about drinking - an unhealthy, ineffective coping style - to help you deal with the problems in your life. No outside substance or activity - booze, food, dieting, cutting, hoarding, etc. - is ever going to transform your hurting inner self into a happy one permanently. A cocktail may take the edge off for an hour or two, but it won't make any lasting changes in your head or your life.

So when you start thinking a vodka tonic is the answer to your problems, talk back. Tell yourself a drink is just a drink. And it won't resolve any important issues or improve the quality of your life long-term. Then start addressing your concerns in healthy ways - instead of hitting the bottle. Deal with external matters directly, not indirectly with a margarita. You'll not only be putting some of your troubles to rest, you'll also be abandoning the notion that alcohol is the solution to them.

Stop suffering - and drinking - in silence! If you assume a more proactive problem-solving approach to life, you'll drink less.

8. Never Lose Your Sense of Self

Your sense of self. Knowing who you are and valuing yourself. Without it, you're an empty shell without meaning, purpose or hope.

If you're so wrapped up in doing for others that you've forgotten who you are and how to take care of your own needs, listen up. Refocus and start taking better care of yourself. You're worth it! When you do, you'll be appreciating yourself and remembering who you are. And the more you know who you are and love yourself, the less interest you'll have in liquor or any other harmful substance or activity for that matter.

Do you know who you are? If you think highly of yourself and take good care of yourself, you won't be attracted to alcohol.

9. Know When the Alcohol is Talking

That dreamy high you get from liquor reinforces your drinking. Yes, you feel relaxed and happy after a pop or two, but it does have its downside. You want to keep on drinking and therein lies the problem.

When you drink, listen to when the wine is talking. It's saying, "If you feel this good after a couple of drinks, you'll feel even better after one more". Then step back, be objective and remind yourself that booze is always trying to talk you into having "just one more". It's the nature of the beast. And even though you're enjoying yourself right now, if you follow its lead and keep on drinking you'll pay the price for it later. The truth is more alcohol won't enhance your high, it will just numb you and get you drunk and you'll feel awful in the morning.

So the next time you're under the influence and the wine is talking to you - telling you to have more and more - come back down to earth, turn off the liquor talk, thank the chardonnay for a very nice time, stop drinking and be on your merry way. Then you'll come out on top - you'll be the winner, not the wine.

One of your greatest challenges will be to stop drinking after you've had a couple. Talk back to alcohol and you'll overcome it!

10. Sensitize Yourself to Feeling Full

You know how satisfied you feel after a great meal? When you're full and not interested in another bite? Cultivate this feeling with spirits too. You might just be content and ready to stop - before you even hit your limit!

After every drink, reflect on how satisfied you feel. Give yourself a five or ten minute breather - without another cocktail - and think about how full you are on just one or two glasses. You might feel comfortable enough to stop at that point. Go with your feelings!

Listen to your body and your brain when you're drinking. They can tell you when it's time to slow down or stop!

11. Stop Overthinking

We, as women, have a tendency to overthink and overanalyze our issues and problems. We look at snags from every possible angle, upside down and inside out, over and over again. We obsess about glitches until it makes us crazy. And we drink while we're fixating.

Give yourself a break once you've thoroughly examined an issue. Stop the mind games and settle on the best course of action for you.

Then follow through with your plans. Obsessing about a problem won't solve it or do you any good. But it might stress you out even more and increase your alcohol consumption.

Think less and stick to your conclusions more and you might not need liquor to stop the merry-go-round spinning around inside of your head. Simplified thinking may lead to lighter drinking!

12. Fine Tune a Take It or Leave It Attitude About Alcohol

Your ultimate goal! When you have a take it or leave it attitude about liquor, you'll always drink sensibly and never go overboard. You won't have to count your drinks or look at the clock to pace yourself. Moderate drinking will be effortless and you'll never worry about it.

The next time you're thinking about having a cocktail, think about how you can live without it instead. A drink is just a drink and not having one - even when you want one - is not the end of the world. You can take it or leave it. Try out this self-talk when you're tempted to imbibe. It's not as hard as you think and you might just say no to drinking for the time being.

Another way to develop a take it or leave it attitude about alcohol is to just leave it - literally. Leave a half-finished drink. When you stop drinking and walk away from a pop before you're done, you're making a powerful statement to yourself. You're saying, "I control alcohol, alcohol does not control me". And it feels so good to be in charge - increasing your self-control and self-confidence around spirits so it's easier for you to refuse in the future.

Eventually, you will internalize this take it or leave it attitude - if you think about it and act on it every time you're considering drinking. And automatic moderate drinking will be yours forever.

13. A Healthy Lifestyle is the Antidote to Problem Drinking

Cravings, including alcohol cravings, may diminish or disappear when you feel good physically. Your mood improves and liquor isn't that appealing to you when you're in the pink. So here are some healthy tips to lift your spirits and curb your desire to drink.

A wholesome, well-balanced diet should be your number one priority. Lots of fruits, vegetables and whole grains, some lean protein and a little dairy should make up most of your diet. A healthy diet keeps your blood sugar levels stable, which also stabilizes your mood and reduces cravings. Fatty, sugary, junk food, on the other hand, wreaks havoc on your blood sugar levels. When you eat junk, they yoyo up and down and so does your mood - triggering cravings.

Physical activity should be another priority. Working out at least three times a week for at least thirty minutes has so many physiological and psychological advantages it's hard to know where to start. You'll lose weight. Your cardiovascular health will improve. Your endorphins - feel good hormones released when you exercise - will explode. And you'll feel fabulous - so you won't need wine to get the job done.

Plenty of rest is next on your healthy lifestyle agenda. Over seventy percent of Americans are sleep deprived and odds are you're one of them, so squeeze in as much shuteye as possible. Go to bed an hour earlier? Stay in bed an hour later? Shoot for at least seven hours a night, more if you can, and you'll feel better, you'll be happier and you'll be less interested in vodka.

Fun is also a must for a healthy lifestyle. You can have the best diet, exercise and sleep regimens in the world, but if you don't have fun, you'll still be susceptible to alcohol abuse. Stepping out with friends, laughing and exploring new hobbies and activities make your life enjoyable. When you're having such a good time, who needs alcohol?

And cultivating a spiritual practice is another aspect of healthy living. Organized or unorganized religion may make your life complete. Getting in touch with your soulful side may not only decrease your need to drink, it may also lead the way to a more fulfilling life in general.

When you feel good physically, you feel good psychologically. And you don't need wine or any other substance to get by. Think about it.

14. Learn to Be Happy - Without Alcohol

Imagine being happy without booze - where you don't need it to feel good or to have fun. You can create a joyful life for yourself - without spirits - and here are a few pointers to do just that.

Start living in the present. Take in each moment and event as they unfold, instead of dwelling on the past or being anxious about the future. If you work on being truly present, you won't waste your time dwelling on negative thoughts and you'll be happier.

Thrive where you are too. That is, put your heart and soul into what you're doing right now. If you're working, do your best work. If you're staying home and taking care of kids, be the best parent you can be. If you're cleaning the house or cooking dinner, give it your all. When you do your best, you feel good about yourself and you make others happy too.

Practice gratitude. So often we focus on the bad things in our lives and we take the good things for granted. When you catch yourself obsessing about the downers in your life, switch to the uppers instead. It will improve your mood. Everyday, think of at least five things you're grateful for. They don't have to be really big or important things. Maybe a good night's rest, a strong cup of coffee, a nice person, an excellent glass of wine and fried chicken could make up your gratitude list for the day. Maybe a hot shower, your kid's smiles, cookies, a thoughtful act and comfortable shoes could make your list. What are you grateful for?

Have meaningful conversations. Research shows that when you talk to good friends about deep subjects, you increase your happiness quotient. Superficial conversation with acquaintances is fine most of the time, but thoughtful talks with people you like and trust are luxuries and will increase your feeling of well-being.

And you can only have meaningful conversations with good friends. People who are nice to you and have your best interests at heart. People who share your thoughts and values for the most part. People who you like being around and enjoy the same interests and activities that you enjoy. Good people who are there for you when times are tough brighten your outlook and your life.

Practice forgiving if you've been wronged. You might not be receptive to the idea at first and you may think it's impossible at times. But when you think about it, the only person you're hurting by holding a grudge is yourself. If you can forgive, you can let go of your hurt and anger. You set yourself free emotionally and make way for more positive feelings.

Smile! When all else fails to make you happy, smile. There are so many advantages to smiling! You look better. You look younger. You're more attractive. Smiling actually makes you happier. It lowers your blood pressure and stress levels and releases feel good chemicals into your system that perk you up. Smiling boosts your immune system too. And it's contagious. When you smile, others smile back at you - making you and everyone around you happier.

You can be joyful without leaning on liquor. Brainstorm all of the ways you can make yourself happier and follow through with them. You'll drink less!

15. And Look at the Big Picture of Your Life . . .

Now look at your life in it's entirety. If you're obsessed about a dream relationship, a dream job, a dream family or a dream lifestyle and it's not materializing, rethink your obsession. Wasting too much of your precious energy fantasizing on how fabulous your life could be if only you had the perfect partner, career, family or standard of living won't get you anywhere - but dissatisfied and perhaps drinking heavily.

Be more realistic about your goals and put them in perspective. Of course, strive for your hopes and dreams - but don't base your happiness on them. Pursue them - but don't depend on them to make your life complete. If you don't place all of your eggs in one basket and have a well-rounded attitude about life, you'll have a healthier lifestyle and mindset and you'll be less interested in alcohol.

Focus on all of the wonderful, fulfilling aspects of your life, instead of daydreaming about unrealistic expectations and ambitions. You'll be a happier - without wine.

Start Thinking and Living Like a Moderate Drinker

1. Balance is the Key to a Moderate Drinking Mentality and Lifestyle
2. Cozy Up to the Concept of Appropriate Drinking
3. Cozy Up to the Concept of Mindful Drinking Too
4. Put Alcohol in Perspective

5. Make Alcohol Less Important in Your Life

6. View Alcohol Realistically

7. Don't Control Your Inner Self with Outside Substances

8. Never Lose Your Sense of Self

9. Know When the Alcohol is Talking

10. Sensitize Yourself to Feeling Full on Alcohol

11. Stop Overthinking!

12. Fine Tune a Take It or Leave It Attitude About Alcohol

13. A Healthy Lifestyle is the Antidote to Problem Drinking

14. Learn to Be Happy - Without Alcohol

15. And Look at the Big Picture of Your Life . . .

Chapter 9

Stop Drinking Your Problems Away - Fix Them!

Y ou've written your story - identifying all of the underlying issues that started you drinking and are keeping you drinking. Now you're going to discover how to handle each and every one of these concerns in healthy ways - instead of resorting to alcohol.

When you follow through with solid plans to resolve your problems, they'll no longer drive you to drink. You'll know you've done your best and you'll be less likely to engage in heavy drinking to cope with them. You'll lead the happy, healthy life you've always envisioned for yourself - minus destructive drinking!

Genetic and Biological Factors

If you think you have a genetic predisposition for alcohol abuse, you should be extra careful about your drinking. If one of your parents is an alcoholic or if you have several family members who are alcoholics, you are at greater risk for developing alcoholism. If you're the child of an alcoholic, you're four to ten times more likely to become an alcoholic, compared to a child who has no close relatives who are alcoholics. You're also more likely to start drinking at a younger age and develop a drinking problem early on. And people with a family history of alcoholism are less likely to outgrow a drinking problem, compared to people with no family history of it. You don't want to fall into the same old problem drinking trap other family members have fallen into, so you really need to keep an eye on your alcohol intake.

You might have a higher tolerance for booze, so you need more of it to get high and that could translate into increased consumption. Or you might be more sensitive to the positive effects of liquor than the average drinker - like feeling more relaxed and comfortable in social settings - which could also reinforce hard drinking. Or you may have engaged in binge drinking when you were young which caused brain damage and led to heavy drinking in adulthood.

If alcohol abuse runs in your family or you have a higher tolerance to spirits than most people or you're more sensitive to the positive effects of alcohol than most drinkers or binge drinking when you were young factors into your drinking problem, take note. No, you may not be able to change your genes, your family history or your reckless drinking past. But you can recognize you're at greater risk for alcoholism and need to be extra vigilant about your alcohol consumption. Always keep those thoughts in the back of your mind - especially when you're drinking. They might keep you on the straight and narrow.

If you think genetic or biological factors have led to your problem drinking . . .

Be honest with yourself about your family history of alcohol abuse

Be aware of other biological factors that may affect your drinking

Remind yourself you're at greater risk for alcoholism

Be extra careful if you do drink

Personality Characteristics

If you think you have certain personality characteristics that trigger your drinking, acknowledge them. If you're more impulsive than most people - you have spontaneous thoughts and act on sudden urges - or you're hyperactive or you're overly interested in thrill-seeking experiences, you can manage these traits so they don't lead to harmful drinking.

First, stop, get a grip and get back to reality. Instead of letting your thoughts and behavior run away with you, chill and take a timeout. That might bring you back to your senses so you don't plunge headfirst into destructive drinking.

Calm down too. Take it easy before giving in to wild and crazy thoughts. More often than not, relaxing and slowing down will help you to determine if your desire to drink is just a passing fancy or something more serious.

Think of the consequences of your actions too. When you think of the outcome of your behavior and what's in your best interest, you might change your mind about doing it. Then you'll be in control of impulsive thoughts and drinking, instead of the other way around.

The same goes for hyperactivity. When you're feeling restless or agitated, take charge, take a break and slow down. Unwind and figure out what's right for you long-term. Risky drinking may seem fun at the time, but you don't want to pay the price for it later.

Organize your thinking and behavior. Well-thought-out actions, instead of giving in to foolish ones, is good advice for anyone trying to manage these pesky personality traits. Preplanning takes the recklessness out of your behavior and allows you to have a good time in a controlled way.

More strategies to beat dangerous impulsive, thrill-seeking or hyperactive thinking that can result in problem drinking? Educate yourself about your personality characteristics. The more you know about them, the less vulnerable you'll be to them. And look into counseling with a mental health professional who specializes in the personality traits you want to get a handle on. Perhaps they could help you to establish a more grounded lifestyle - which might decrease your alcohol consumption. If all else fails, consider prescription medication. It might settle you down and put the brakes on unsafe thinking and behavior.

If you can relate to any one of these personality characteristics and you drink, listen up. The good news is if you know they influence your alcohol use, you can take steps to cancel them and your problem drinking out!

If you think personality characteristics have led to your problem drinking ...

Stop and get a grip

Relax and slow down

Think of the consequences of your actions

Organize your thoughts and behavior

Educate yourself about your personality characteristics

Get professional help

Consider prescription medication

Family Influences

If you think the attitudes and habits you learned at home about drinking and alcohol have shaped your current drinking habits, recognize them. Then, and only then, can you challenge them and replace them with healthy new ones.

Odds are your drinking mirrors your parent's patterns of alcohol use or abuse. From an early age, you learned from their example - when to drink, why to drink, how to drink and how much to drink. If your parents were smart, sensible drinkers, lucky you! Hopefully, you've modeled your drinking habits after theirs and picked up their moderate drinking ways. But if they were alcohol abusers, you most likely learned their bad habits and picked up their problem drinking ways.

You probably internalized your parent's beliefs and expectations about liquor too. If they drank appropriately - when eating or socializing - you learned that wine was a nice accompaniment to a meal or a special occasion. But if they drank inappropriately, you may have latched on to the notion that booze was a cure-all for feelings and problems. In fact, you might have acquired all sorts of strange beliefs and expectations about drinking and alcohol - like drinking everyday for no good reason is acceptable or Saturday night is drunk night - that you carry with you to this day.

Compare your parent's drinking habits and attitudes to yours. If you inherited their unhealthy, inappropriate attitudes, behaviors and beliefs, delete them immediately. Then make way for wholesome, appropriate ones. Goodbye old problem drinking patterns, hello sensible new ones!

If you think family influences have led to your problem drinking . . .

Examine the drinking attitudes and behaviors you learned at home

Examine the beliefs and expectations about alcohol you learned at home

Compare your current drinking habits and attitudes to your parents

Delete old, problem drinking habits, attitudes, beliefs and expectations

Make way for healthy new ones

Childhood Abuse and Trauma

If you think sexual, emotional or physical abuse or trauma you suffered as a child factors into your drinking, deal with it. Admitting abuse happened is an important first step to healing it. If you can't accept that it took place, you can't fix it and you'll continue to cope with it in destructive ways - like drinking too much. But once you recognize that the abuse and the harmful behaviors you've developed to deal with it are just diversions keeping you from your truth, you'll start the healing process.

Rejecting personal responsibility for the mistreatment is the next step to recovering from it. Even though you had nothing to do with it and you weren't to blame for it, you might have feelings of guilt and shame. You may think you somehow caused it. And your abuser may have blamed you for their actions and told you that it was your fault and you deserved it. Now is the time to talk back to that kind of thinking. You were born a perfect, innocent child and deserved a happy childhood - free from any type of exploitation. You never deserved it and you don't share any responsibility for it.

Once you've admitted the problem and stopped blaming yourself for it, you must forgive yourself. But forgiving yourself and healing from childhood abuse rarely happens on your own or in isolation. Talking freely about your experiences in a safe environment should be the next step in your recovery. The understanding and support of individuals who have gone through similar ordeals will help you to get past it. You'll realize you can forgive others who have been victimized, so it's possible to forgive yourself too. Check out support groups for childhood abuse survivors in your area. Ask your physician, clergyman, counselor or psychologist for referrals. And if groups don't work for you, try connecting with a mental health professional who specializes in childhood abuse recovery. Working through these crucial issues with a qualified mental health specialist will get you on the right track.

If you're still haunted by a traumatic event in your childhood, stop sweeping it under the rug. You don't want an upsetting experience when you were young, like the death of a parent, a serious illness or living in extreme poverty, to dictate your drinking behavior for the rest of your life. So instead of continuing to live with the sadness or anger of a stressful event, express your feelings. The sooner you get them out in the open - in a support group or with professional counseling - the sooner you'll get control of your drinking and your life.

Now you're ready to leave the painful past behind and move on. Remember - you are not defined by what happened to you years ago. And negative experiences that you can't do anything about are long over. But you can do something about your future - and make it better. Clean your psychological house and you'll make way for a healthier, happier life - no longer relying on alcohol to help you deal with horrible childhood episodes.

Also, educate yourself about childhood abuse and trauma - how it can affect one's life and how it has affected yours personally. The more you know about how it has influenced your relationships and your path, the less impact it will have on you.

Hopefully, throughout the recovery process you'll connect with people who treat you well. In fact, one of your goals as a childhood abuse survivor is to surround yourself with positive, supportive people who bring out the best in you, instead of toxic ones who bring you down.

On your own or with the help of a support group or therapist, you can leave the hurt behind, your need to drink will fade and you'll move on to the beautiful new life you deserve.

If you think childhood abuse or trauma has led to your problem drinking . . .

Admit it

Reject personal responsibility for it

Forgive yourself

Express yourself with the support of others

Consider professional counseling

Remember you are not defined by your past

Leave the painful past behind

Educate yourself about childhood abuse and it's effects

Connect with positive people who treat you well

Move on to the beautiful new life you deserve

Traditional Roles

If you dislike or have trouble fulfilling the traditional women's roles you may have been born into, you might be using liquor to cope with your dissatisfaction. Women's roles have been changing and evolving for the last one hundred and fifty years - from the traditional stay-at-home wife and mother to superwoman. And coming terms with or trying to manage all of your different roles, expectations and responsibilities may be driving you to drink.

The traditional woman's role dictates you stay at home and be supportive and nurturing to your partner and children. You're the selfless caretaker of the family - you cook, clean and tend to everyone's physical and psychological needs. You put everyone else first and love unconditionally.

Then came feminism and the equal rights and equal pay movements for women. Women were encouraged to get out in the world, work outside of the home and to share parenting and household chores with men. They were told they could have it all. You could not only be a wife and mother, but a successful career woman too. And the superwoman was born. The superwoman has a partner, raises children, keeps the house and helps support the family. She now has so many roles and obligations she doesn't know if she's coming or going.

Some women strive to be superwoman and have it all. Some women prefer to be the traditional stay-at-home wife, mother and homemaker. And some women focus solely on their careers - minus a partner or family. Today, endless variations on women's roles - both traditional and non-traditional - exist.

If you reject some or all of these roles or you're confused about your identity and still trying to figure it out, you may be hitting the bottle to get by. If your identity and roles are changing or you're not enjoying what you're doing and you wish you could be or do something different, you may be hitting the bottle to get by. Or if you're hanging on by a thread - barely able to handle all of your roles and responsibilities and you're unhappy - you may be hitting the bottle to get by.

Here are a few tips to deal with identity and role dissatisfaction, confusion or rejection. Start by defining yourself - as a person, a partner and a mother. What do you think is required of you for each of these roles and what are you willing to give to fulfill them? Being clear on who you are and your job description will eliminate a lot of confusion for you and your loved ones.

Rethink your roles and identity too. If you're not happy with what you're doing, ask yourself how you could change or redefine yourself so you could be. Maybe you're tired of staying at home and want to go back to work, maybe you're tired of working and want to stay at home, maybe you want to devote more time to your career, maybe you want to devote more time to your children. Think about how you can redesign your life so you can do what you really want to do and be who you really want to be. Sometimes we need to reinvent ourselves and our lives and maybe this is your time.

If you're a stay-at-home wife and mother and need a bit more out-side stimulation, look into activities that get you out of the house and into a different zone. Classes, volunteering, a part-time job? Think about your options, think about what you'd enjoy doing and follow through with expanding yourself with extracurricular activities that will get you involved and interested.

If you're superwoman and stretched with family, house and job obligations, shed some. Ask your partner and kids for more help around the house. Or hire a housekeeper, nanny or cook if you can afford it. If possible, reduce your hours at work. Take a day off in the middle of the week, work seven hours a day instead of eight, work from home a couple of days a week. If you can't keep up your current pace and find it impossible to be your best, you need to cut back.

Also, keep in mind there are limits to what you can give. And when people ask too much of you, you've got to draw the line. You have to say no to family, friends and employers at times to survive. Setting limits will make you an even better person, partner, parent and employee. And it will lighten your load.

If you're overwhelmed with health, education and relationship issues concerning your partner, kids or aging parents, get support. Most women feel they're responsible for the health and well-being of their entire family which can be a heavy burden. Consider getting professional help for problems that are wearing you down - get kids into child care or look into marriage counseling or organize assisted living for elderly parents. Let experts do their jobs, instead of you assuming the responsibility for everyone's welfare.

And try not to lose your sense of self - which is easy to do when you're everything to everyone. You're so busy doing for others you might forget who you are and what you're about. Remember - when your needs are met, you're happier and you're a better wife, mother and employee. So you need to take care of yourself before you can be your best for others.

If you're unhappy with your roles and life, redesign them and make adjustments so you can be happy. Then you'll no longer need alcohol to see you through.

If you think your identity and roles have led to your problem drinking . . .

Define your identity and roles and their expectations

Rethink your roles and identity

Revise your roles to your liking

Set limits

Learn to say no

Get help and support from others

Take good care of yourself

Relationships

If you have difficult relationships with your parents, partner, kids, friends or colleagues, and they increase your desire to drink, now's the time to take them on. If you don't, and you continue to let them upset you, you might not be able to fix your drinking problem.

Relationships with parents are pretty much set in stone. Your parent's attitudes and behavior patterns and your reactions to them have been going on for years and it would probably take nothing short of a miracle for any of you to change. You can try to air your concerns about the relationship with them on your own or you might consider professional family counseling to work through problems. Or you can lower your expectations of the relationship. If you don't expect too much, you won't be disappointed. Or you can stop focusing on the relationship. If you stop investing so much time and energy on trying to make it right, it will become less important to you.

If your relationship with your partner isn't the greatest, sort out the reasons behind the strife. Take a step back and a good hard look at what's led to the breakdown. Once you've identified the troubling issues, dream up ways you can both work on them to mend the union. And commit to changing your attitudes and behaviors if you think it will improve your time together.

Look at both of your drinking habits too, as well as codependent and enabling behaviors you engage in. Analyze your drinking triggers and responses and understand how they lead to problem drinking when

117

you're together. What feelings, issues or circumstances cause overdrinking when you're partying with your significant other? Be specific. Talk to your mate about these cues before either one of you has a drop to drink and brainstorm ways you can change your behavior patterns around booze. Then follow through with them.

If you're with a heavy drinking partner who encourages your drinking or you both feed off of each other's bad drinking habits, you've got to manage the relationship so spirits no longer factor in. Get smart and read up on enabling and codependent behaviors. The more you know about them, the less susceptible you'll be to them - promoting a healthier connection and less imbibing for both of you.

Enlisting your partner's participation and support in a moderate drinking program might also be a brilliant move to help both of you control your drinking and improve your relationship. Getting your spouse on board and working the program together might be the best strategy for you to cut down and be happier. Toss the idea out to your mate.

If you're staying together for the kid's sake or for financial reasons or because it's convenient, you may be drinking just to cope. When you feel "stuck" with no change or improvement in sight, the euphoria of alcohol gives you a break from those hopeless feelings. Unfortunately, when you turn to booze to escape or lift your spirits, that's when addiction happens. So it's up to you to either pursue options to improve your situation or to stop drinking altogether.

If your partnership still isn't working, get marriage counseling. Couples counseling that focuses on communication, control, trust, feelings, self-esteem, inappropriate behavior, responsibility, resolving conflict and how to give and receive love might do the trick. Maybe that would end the bad blood and hard drinking between you and your significant other.

But if your partner isn't interested in investing the time or energy in counseling to better the relationship, maybe you should consider moving on. Some people and relationships are toxic and you may have no choice but to start anew. Love does have limits and separation or divorce might be reasonable options. Forgive yourself for the part you played in the ill-fated union and look to the future. Trying to make a relationship work when it's impossible might just turn you into an alcoholic.

If kids, friends, colleagues or blended families are getting under your skin, try to pinpoint and address the issues that are driving you wild. Don't just sit, simmer and sip. Detach and be cool when presenting concerns to others and encourage everyone to come up with solutions to problems that are making you unhappy. Or, again, lower your expectations of the relationship. Or stop paying so much attention to the people and the sore spots. If you can make unhealthy people and connections less important to you, they'll bother you less. In some cases, you might want to cut your losses and stop associating with a difficult individual or terminate a doomed relationship.

Empowering yourself may also help you to break a problem drinking pattern you've developed while struggling with relationship issues. First, acknowledge your negative feelings, like inequality, powerlessness, fear and anger and other symptoms, like headaches, overeating, fatigue and depression, caused by an unhealthy association. Then recognize your wise, compassionate and loving self. And pamper yourself - physically, mentally and spiritually. You'll increase your self-esteem and self-confidence. When you think positively about yourself, you might feel powerful enough to elevate or eliminate the relationship - instead of remaining dissatisfied and letting it drag on.

Cultivating your personal power on your own may be possible, but if that doesn't work consider joining a woman's empowerment group or get into individual therapy with a mental health professional who specializes in women's issues. When you feel strong and confident, you'll have better relationships, you'll be better relationship material, you'll attract better relationship material and you won't need wine to drink your relationship problems away.

The bottom line is if you're drinking too much because of faulty connections, you've got to change something - yourself, the situation or both. And if you follow through with positive changes, you'll probably follow through with moderate drinking too.

If you think relationship issues have led to your problem drinking . . .

Pinpoint problems in the relationship

Air your concerns with the people involved

Detach and be cool when discussing relationship issues

Brainstorm solutions to problems and follow through

Lower your expectations of the relationship

Stop focusing on the people and the relationship

Identify codependent and enabling behaviors in the relationship

Commit to change

Work the moderate drinking program with your partner

Consider couples counseling

End the relationship

Empower yourself

Join a women's support group

Seek professional counseling

Change yourself, the situation or both to improve the relationship

Low Self-Esteem

If you don't feel good about yourself and think low self-esteem plays into your drinking, come to terms with it. Your thoughts and perceptions of yourself, how other people treat you and react to you, your relationships with your parents, siblings, peers, teachers and other important contacts, your experiences at home, school, work and in the community, illness, disability or injury, culture, religion and your role and status in society can all make or break your self-worth - and shape your drinking behavior.

The best advice to increase your self-esteem? Start by leading a healthy lifestyle. When you take care of yourself you're saying, "I matter and I'm worth it". And you feel better about yourself already. You're also setting the stage to improve other important aspects of your life that will enhance your self-worth. So eat right, exercise and get plenty of rest.

Spoil yourself psychologically too. Savor your successes and accomplishments and give yourself credit for them. Recognize all of the good things you do everyday - big things and little things - and give yourself a pat on the back for them. Stay upbeat too - look on the bright side and remind yourself of all the things that have gone well. And instead of obsessing about your flaws and weaknesses, obsess about your talents and superior qualities. When you pamper yourself psychologically, you're building healthy self-esteem. So stay positive and appreciate all of the wonderful things you do everyday. You'll like yourself more.

Set realistic, achievable goals for yourself. If you place unreasonable demands on yourself or you aim too high, you set yourself up for failure and disappointment. But if you have realistic expectations and goals and you achieve them, you boost your self-worth. Accomplish reasonable goals and you'll think more of yourself.

Your thoughts and perceptions of yourself probably have the greatest impact on how much you value yourself and the good news is you can control these thoughts. The first step to overcoming negative thoughts, feelings and thinking patterns that are keeping you and your self-esteem down is to identify them. All-or-nothing-at-all thinking - where there is no in-between, mental filtering - where you only see the bad stuff and concentrate on it, not being realistic - where you distort a situation, converting positives into negatives - where you reject your achievements by saying they don't count, jumping to conclusions - where you have little or no evidence to support a negative conclusion, mistaking feelings for facts - where you confuse feelings or beliefs with facts and self put-downs - where you downplay yourself even when you succeed at something - are all devaluing feeling and thought patterns. And they mess with the positive perception of yourself.

Once you've identified the counterproductive emotions and beliefs that are holding you back, you can manage them so they don't step on your self-worth. First, when negative thoughts and self-talk pass through your mind, challenge them. How accurate are these thoughts? Ask yourself if these notions are consistent with facts and logic or if other explanations might be plausible. Question long-held beliefs about yourself that make you feel bad too. They may feel normal, but they aren't. They could just be ideas not based on reason or commonsense.

Then counter and replace devaluing self-talk. Talk back to inaccurate thoughts and replace them with accurate, constructive thoughts instead. Also, use hopeful statements, instead of pessimistic ones. Rethink upsetting thoughts too. If an upsetting thought about you comes up, ask yourself what you can think or do to make the thought less stressful. Rethinking and replacing negative feelings and beliefs about yourself with positive ones will help you to control how you think about yourself. And you'll develop stronger self-esteem.

Bad things that have happened in the past and make you think less of yourself are behind you now. Forgive yourself for the mistakes you've made and don't dwell on them. Poor decisions you made long ago should not affect your present or future. Then move forward with a clean slate - acknowledging your wonderful self that's just waiting to be revealed. Another great strategy to strengthen your self-worth.

Remember, at your core you are perfect. You were born that way. And even though you may err at times - we all do - you're a decent human being. Always treat yourself with kindness and respect because you're entitled to it. Own this attitude and you'll own greater self-esteem.

Surround yourself with supportive people too. If your relationships are strong and healthy, you'll generally receive positive feedback about yourself and have better self-esteem. But if you're running with the wrong crowd, you probably get negative feedback - you might be criticized, teased or disrespected by others - and your self-worth suffers. You should rethink relationships with people who put you down. They don't do a thing for you or your self-esteem. But hanging with interesting, intelligent people who respect you and treat you well, on the other hand, will build your self-worth.

Improving your perception of yourself, controlling your thinking about yourself and increasing the positive feelings you have about yourself will stoke your self-esteem - and prevent destructive drinking.

If you think low self-esteem has led to your problem drinking . . .

Take good care of yourself

Spoil yourself psychologically

Give yourself credit for your successes and accomplishments

Acknowledge the good things you do everyday

Highlight the positive aspects of your life

Focus on your good qualities, not your flaws

Set realistic, achievable goals for yourself

Don't place unreasonable demands on yourself that can't be met

Identify negative feelings, thoughts and thinking patterns about yourself

Control your self-talk and perception of yourself

Challenge and talk back to negative thoughts about yourself

Replace negative thoughts and feelings about yourself with positive ones

Forgive yourself for past mistakes

Move forward with a clean slate

Always remember that at your core you are a perfect human being

Surround yourself with thoughtful, supportive people who are nice to you

Depression

If you suffer from depression - you're sad or unhappy for an extended period of time - and you think it's at the root of your drinking problem, acknowledge it. Then apply these tips - better coping skills - to help you beat the blues and the harmful drinking that accompanies them.

The first thing you should do is to admit you're depressed. Don't deny it, sweep it under the rug, try to wait it out or pretend it will go away.

The sooner you own up to being unhappy, the sooner you can do something about it.

Next, pinpoint the issues behind it. The clearer you are about what's making you sad, the better. Family problems? Money problems? Health problems? Relationship problems? Work problems? School problems? Feeling stuck? Identify the specific feelings, people, circumstances or situations that are causing your unhappiness and you'll be one step closer to happiness.

What can you change about your life to elevate your mood? Brain-storming different solutions to problems that are bringing you down is the next step. Get creative and dream up ways to eliminate or alleviate each of your concerns. Then put your best plans into action. And if they don't work, move on to others. Eventually, you'll hit on the right solutions and feel more upbeat.

Some problems might require help - a support group, a community, mental health or social services agency, a marriage, family and child counselor, a financial counselor, an employment counselor, a mental health professional, a doctor or a lawyer. Don't be afraid to ask for help if it will ease your depression.

And unfortunately, some problems have no clear-cut solutions. In that case, you have to change the way you perceive them or think about them. You can allow them to be the centerpiece of your life and let them eat away at you. Or you can minimize them or write them off - so they no longer depress you. You may not be able to change or control a problem, but you can change or control the way you think about a problem - which puts you in charge and relieves feelings of helpless depression. An attitude adjustment about difficult issues may be your only option to managing them - and your sadness.

If events from your past are making you melancholy, it's time to let go of them. What's done is done and you can't change the past, but you don't have to be defined by it for the rest of your life. Pardon yourself for the mistakes you've made, then move on and be the best you can be in the future.

Identify thought patterns that make you blue too. Tune in to negative thoughts and self-talk that make you sad and when you're having them, just stop. Replace them with positive statements instead. If you challenge downer self-talk, you'll stop thinking like a depressed person!

Adhere to a regular health regimen. Make sure to eat right, get plenty of rest and lots of exercise. Exercise in particular has been proven to be just as effective as prescription medication to treat depression! When you're in the dumps, walk, run, play tennis, go to the gym, whatever. A healthy lifestyle will do wonders for your attitude.

Be proactive. Taking action feels so much better than letting depression have it's way with you. If you're unhappy because you're bored or lonely, make a point of getting out and into activities you enjoy. Socialize with people of like mind, take a class, go dancing, join a club, start a club, have lunch with friends. Get involved. Get creative. Living life to the fullest every day will chase away despair.

Fine tune a better attitude to help you overcome obstacles in life. If that relationship didn't work out or you didn't get that promotion, don't sit at home, mope and drink. Keep moving forward - no matter what - and don't let anyone or anything hold you back. Put your best foot forward and the clouds will lift.

Forgive others. Easier said than done sometimes. Just imagine letting go of all the negative feelings you harbor towards others and how free you'd feel if you did. What a relief - you'd no longer be emotionally bound to people and events that have made you so sad for so long. Forgive others and you'll be happier.

Have fun. You can't be depressed when you're enjoying yourself! What are your favorite activities? Plan on at least one fun activity a day to defeat the doldrums. It may be something as simple as telling jokes or eating an ice cream cone. You'll notice an improvement in your attitude immediately.

Talk about your feelings. Getting negative feelings off your chest is a terrific way to let go of them so you can get on with your life. You can casually talk to friends about what's bothering you. Or maybe you have a trusted friend you can pour your heart out to. Talking about your feelings is a blues buster.

Cultivate a mind/body practice. Try meditation, yoga, tai chi or another spiritual tradition to raise your spirits. Get involved in a mind/body practice and you'll enjoy a mini-vacation from melancholy.

Explore alternative medicine. If you're into herbal remedies, St. John's Wort has been used to treat depression for centuries. And extensive clinical research indicates it's just as effective as prescription anti-depressant medication. Make sure you talk to your physician before trying any herbal remedy, especially if you're taking any other drugs or if you have any other health or psychological problems.

Consider counseling. You'll feel better sooner rather than later with the support and guidance of a mental health professional specializing in the treatment of depression. Their care and expertise could give you the edge and you'd stop wasting your precious time feeling bad. Your physician or clergyman should be able to give you referrals. The talking cure really works.

As a last resort, think about prescription medication. If all else fails, it might bring you up. And anti-depressants combined with psychological counseling is a dynamic duo that has been proven to decimate depression.

Depression is a drag and can lead to alcohol abuse. Addressing it now, instead of waiting and hoping it passes, is the smart thing to do. You'll avoid years of unhappiness and unhealthy drinking if you do.

If you think depression has led to your problem drinking . . .

Acknowledge depression

Pinpoint the issues behind it

Brainstorm different solutions to resolve the issues

Put your depression-busting plans to work

Ask for help

Change the way you perceive and think about issues that depress you

Minimize issues that make you unhappy and you can't change

Let go of issues that make you unhappy and you can't change

Forgive yourself for mistakes you've made in the past

Keep moving forward

Challenge negative feelings and self-talk that fuel
your depression

Take good care of yourself physically

Exercise

Be proactive and pursue activities you enjoy

Socialize with people you like

Get involved in living

Get out and have fun

Develop a better attitude to overcome obstacles in
life

Forgive others

Talk about your feelings

Cultivate a spiritual practice

Explore alternative medicine remedies

Consider professional counseling

Consider prescription medication

Stress

If stress is whetting your appetite for alcohol, relieve it. Feeling you're pushed to the limit not only takes a physical and psychological toll on you, it can lead to problem drinking too. But you can reduce and control your stress so it doesn't trigger dangerous drinking. And here are some pointers - better coping skills - to help you to do just that.

First, you have to recognize it. If you deny you're stressed and insist there's nothing wrong, you can't fix it. Being straight with yourself and admitting you're tense is the first step to overcoming it. And knowing your reactions to stress may be just as important as admitting it. Do you drink too much, eat too much or smoke too much when you're under the gun? Do you get headaches, backaches, feel angry, anxious or out of control when you're under pressure? Think about it.

Next, identify the issues that are stressing you out. Family? Money? Work? Juggling family, household and professional obligations all at the same time? Not enough time in the day to get everything done? You have to pinpoint your stressors before you can get a handle on them.

Now dream up ways to manage these concerns so they don't get to you. Focus on healthy coping skills, not unhealthy ones - like using alcohol to drink them away. If maintaining the family, household and your job are too much for you, look for ways to lighten up. Start with a family meeting and talk about what others can do to pitch in. Or hire help for household duties if you can afford it. Talk to your employer about working less or working from home. And tweak your schedule to give yourself a little extra wiggle room during the day. Devising a plan to de-stress and sticking to it is a healthier way to deal with it than swilling vodka.

Set realistic goals and expectations for yourself. When you overdo it and shoot for the moon, you might not make it. And that stresses you out even more. Prioritize your duties too. Get the most important things done first, then go down your list. You might not get everything done you want to get done. That's okay. But you'll get to the most important stuff and you'll take care of the rest later. Also, give yourself plenty of time to complete your chores. When you're pressed for time, stress mounts. And communicate assertively and effectively. Learn to say no to obligations and people who want you to assume more work and responsibility. Everyone will know where you stand, what you're committed to and what your limits are. There won't be any confusion about what your commitment is - and you'll stress less.

If at first you don't succeed at de-stressing your life, try, try again. If one solution for eliminating pressure doesn't work, move on to the next and keep trying different solutions until you hit on ones that do. Hopefully, over time the stressors and tension will fade and you'll feel better.

Step back and look at your demands in a different light too. Rethinking the way you perceive some people and circumstances might reduce the strain. Some problems simply can't be fixed, but you can change the way you think about them or perceive them. You can choose to let them get under your skin or you can look at them from a less stressful viewpoint. Looking at your stressors objectively and from different angles may defuse them and your stress level.

Remind yourself that nothing is the end of the world. Life goes on - no matter what. Putting stressors in their place and minimizing the role they play in your life is another trick to dealing with them. Downplay them and they won't weigh you down.

128

And some circumstances are beyond your control and trying to change your mind about them doesn't even work. At that point, perhaps the best approach for you is to simply accept the situation, leave it behind and move on with your life. Acceptance might be the secret to you feeling more relaxed.

Rethink your values and what's most important to you too. Concentrate on what really matters to you - good health, family, friends, being a good person, partner or parent, taking care of your loved ones, giving back to the community. Other things you might be stressing about - putting a pool in the backyard, making all of the kid's soccer games, squeezing in an extra hour or two at work - are really minor concerns in the big picture of your life. Remembering what's most important to you might be the key to calming you down.

Love yourself. Exercise, drink lots of water, enjoy a wholesome diet with lots of fruits, vegetables and whole grains and sleep at least seven hours every night. Exercise specifically is a real stress buster. Make a point of getting more physical activity and you'll be too tired to be stressed.

Also, pump up your self-esteem and self-confidence. When you feel good about yourself, you feel confident you can handle anything that comes your way - including stress and stressors. So the better you feel about yourself, the less susceptible you'll be to pressure.

Make time for people and activities you enjoy. Fun and stress don't mix. When life is getting to you, go out and have a good time with people you like. Blowing off steam with fun people and activities will alleviate tension - guaranteed.

Laugh your stress away. Joking about people and circumstances that get to you is therapeutic. Finding the humor in your stressors helps you to put them in their place and makes them more manageable - and less stressful.

Cultivate a positive, practical attitude about living. Looking on the bright side never stressed anyone out. But looking on the dark side did. Remain upbeat through tough times and you'll not only survive, you'll thrive - peacefully.

Investigate stress reduction strategies and techniques to settle you down. Deep breathing, muscle relaxation, meditation, biofeedback, spiritual training. You might discover a whole new relaxing world out there.

Talk to someone you trust about your stress. A friend who's a good listener and can offer helpful suggestions. Or a mental health professional specializing in stress reduction who can give you the support and guidance you need to chill. Talk about your stress and stressors and you'll feel more tranquil naturally.

The sooner you challenge your stress, the sooner you'll get back to being your serene old self who doesn't need alcohol to unwind.

If you think stress has led to your problem drinking . . .

Acknowledge your stress

Recognize stress-related symptoms

Identify your stressors

Brainstorm healthy solutions to stressors

If one solution doesn't work, move on to another

Set realistic goals and expectations for yourself

Prioritize your tasks

Give yourself plenty of time to get things done

Communicate clearly and assertively

Learn to say no

Look at your stressors in a different light

Minimize and downplay your stressors

Accept unsolvable stressors and move on

Rethink your values and what's really important in
 your life

Commit to a healthy lifestyle

Exercise

Strengthen your self-esteem and self-confidence

Get out, get active and have fun

Laugh at your stressors

Cultivate a positive attitude about living

Research stress reduction strategies and techniques

Talk to friends about your stress

Consider professional counseling to reduce stress

Feelings, Moods and Mental Health Conditions

The sooner you become aware of the connections between certain feelings, moods and mental conditions and your drinking, the easier it will be for you to cut down. How do emotions and states of mind factor into your alcohol use? Tackle this problem and you'll be closer to tackling your drinking.

Sensitizing yourself to the relationship between your feelings and behavior is not that difficult. Start by simply paying attention to your thoughts, emotions, sensations and memories. Then observe your reactions to them. You'll not only gain a deeper insight into how your moods and habits are linked, you'll also gain a deeper understanding of yourself.

What feelings get you drinking? Negative ones like anger, frustration, shame, guilt, powerlessness, feeling stuck or that you have no control over your life? Or positive ones like excitement, satisfaction, feeling proud about an accomplishment or being in love? Or do you drink in response to both positive and negative emotions? Knowing what feelings push your buttons will help you to conquer reactive drinking.

Once you've identified the emotions that spark your alcohol appe-
tite, then identify and address the issues behind them. You can't change problems you don't acknowledge, so acknowledge them. What people, places, situations, circumstances or events stir emotions in you that increase your desire to drink?

Next, address these concerns in constructive ways so they don't lead to emotional problem drinking. If you imbibe when you're angry or frustrated, try to improve the situation causing these negative feelings. Or chill out and distract yourself with a pleasant activity that will take your mind off of being upset. Or learn to accept the situation so it's no longer a risky drinking cue for you. If you drink because you feel ashamed or guilty, make amends, forgive yourself and move on. You can choose to obsess about your past bad behavior and become an alcoholic or you can resolve to do better in the future and not use liquor to cope. If you drink when you're excited, replace beer with fun alcohol-free entertainment. And tell yourself that boozing when you're all worked up is not a healthy or appropriate response to your feelings. If you drink when you're happy, allow yourself a drink or two, but remind yourself that overdoing it won't make you so happy in the morning.

Earlier, you learned how to control internal and external drinking cues that increased your alcohol craving and consumption. This is a good time to refer back to those strategies and techniques to neutralize feelings and moods that might result in drinking. It's also crucial for you to get the heart of the matter, analyze the issues that lead to the emotions that trigger your drinking and either resolve them, weaken them or accept them so you'll stop trying to drink them away.

Remember - plans to deal with alcohol-triggering feelings and moods that are never put to use are meaningless. They're just a collection of words. But when you put plans into action, you give them meaning and you can change your life. Proactively follow through with positive ways of dealing with emotions, instead of drinking. It might be the secret to your moderate drinking success long-term.

Here are a few more pointers to help you handle feelings that get you in trouble. Slow down and think carefully about what you're doing and saying. Also, try to be logical, instead of letting your emotions take over. Keep your head and you'll be less likely to go off the deep end. And step back and put the situation in perspective. The more balanced your thinking is, the less likely you'll have a strong emotional reaction to an unpleasant person or situation and take refuge in wine.

When your feelings are running high, relax. Take a time-out and try deep breathing. Or repeat a calming word or phrase to yourself, such as "calm down" or "relax". Or visualize a tranquil setting, like an empty beach or dense forest. Or engage in a simple, non-strenuous exercise, like yoga, to settle down.

Anxiety - extreme fear or worry - may also cause you to engage in destructive drinking. You might use alcohol to sedate yourself when you're nervous. There are other ways to calm yourself without spirits. Exercise and leading a healthy lifestyle is an obvious solution. Yes, eating right and getting physical not only alleviates stress and depression, it can also lower your anxiety level. And avoid caffeine. If you're nervous to begin with, overdosing on caffeine will only exacerbate the problem. Limit your caffeine intake and you'll limit your anxiety. Caffeine is not only in coffee, it's in tea and many soft and energy drinks as well.

Challenge anxiety-provoking thoughts too. Dwelling on negative thoughts is a recipe for disaster - and anxiety. When you have stomach-churning thoughts, identify them, step back, consciously stop thinking them and replace them with positive ones. For example, if you're anticipating going to the dentist and you think of all the times you've been tortured in the dentist's chair, stop. Then think about the painkillers and the laughing gas the dentist will give you instead. You've just reduced your anxiety level! Replace anxiety-provoking thoughts with positive ones and you won't be so antsy.

Study up on relaxation strategies and techniques. Tackle your fears with deep breathing, muscle relaxation, meditation or soothing music. Learn about biofeedback to control your anxiety. Look into nutritional or herbal supplements to chill. Talk to friends or a mental health professional about your anxiety - what causes it and ways to deal with it. Perhaps hypnosis or hypnotherapy would put you more at ease.

Other mental health conditions may also trigger heavy drinking. If you suffer from Adult Deficit Hyperactivity Disorder, ADHD, or Obsessive-Compulsive Disorder, OCD, or Bipolar Disorder, it's important for you to get help from a mental health professional specializing in the condition you're dealing with. They can shed some light on your situation and offer you an effective treatment plan to handle it. The talking cure might be the answer to your mood or mental health condition. Or prescription medication might make you right. A mental health professional or medication or both might help you to address and relieve your condition. Then you'd no longer need liquor to feel normal.

Get a grip on your feelings, moods or mental health conditions in healthy ways and you'll get a grip on light, problem-free drinking.

If you think feelings, moods or a mental health condition have led to your problem drinking . . .

Sensitize yourself to your feelings

Observe your reactions to your feelings

Identify feelings, moods or mental states that trigger your drinking

Identify the issues behind those feelings and moods

Make plans to deal with those issues in healthy ways

Follow through with your plans

Slow down and think carefully before you react

Keep your head and be logical

Step back and put your feelings in perspective

Balanced thinking will neutralize your emotions

Take a time out and calm down

Acknowledge anxiety and the issues that trigger it

Cultivate a healthy lifestyle and get lots of exercise

Replace anxiety-provoking thoughts with positive ones

Practice relaxation strategies and techniques

Consider alternative medicine remedies

Consider hypnosis or hypnotherapy

Talk about your feelings

Consider professional help for specific mental health conditions

Consider prescription medication for mental health conditions

Peer Pressure

If friends, family or colleagues coerce you into drinking, it's time to think for yourself. You don't want to develop a drinking problem just because other drinkers want you to keep up with them!

Who encourages your drinking? Old friends you've grown up with and have always gotten loaded with? New friends who bring out the bottle whenever you're around? People you work with? Relatives who always have a beer in their hand? Your partner who thinks you connect better after a martini or two? If drinking is expected and overdoing it is acceptable with certain people you associate with, you've actually got two problems: a drinking problem and a social problem. And you need to know who supports your heavy drinking before you can correct either one.

Maybe you drink to fit in, be more popular or to prove yourself. Or you join in so you won't be criticized for not drinking. Look at the reasons why you cave in to peer pressure and go along with the crowd. Knowing why you go with the flow might weaken your drinking response.

Rethink your position if you're drinking to please others too. Your happiness does not depend on using alcohol to impress other people. Or it shouldn't. So if you drink because you're sensitive to what other's think of you or you base your self-worth on other's perceptions of you, stop. There are other ways to feel good about yourself and earn people's approval that don't involve guzzling. Keep that in mind the next time you think you have to do shots to prove yourself.

And at the very least, you'll have to re-evaluate your relationships with friends, family or colleagues who always want you to imbibe with them. If the only thing you have in common with these people is drinking and liquor, putting an end to the relationship is not a great loss. They really don't have your best interests at heart if they want you to abuse alcohol with them. And leading a healthy lifestyle is so much more important to you than trying to maintain unhealthy relationships that revolve around alcohol with problem drinkers.

If cutting ties doesn't work for you, try limiting the time you spend with people who egg you on. Instead of partying endlessly with them like you use to, limit yourself to one or two hours. You might prevent a big blowout - but still preserve your friendship.

135

You could also try to change the focus of the relationship and explain to them you're watching your drinking these days. You could tell them about the moderate drinking program you're working and ask them if they'd be interested in cutting down too. Wouldn't it be great if you could both work the program together? And enjoy safe social drinking together? You could also suggest alcohol-free activities to participate in - instead of drinking. You could go bowling or to the movies. It's worth a try.

Making new friends who aren't big boozers and getting involved in entertainment that doesn't require drinking will also take the pressure off of you. You can have fun without beer! Drinking less would be so much easier if you enjoyed activities that didn't include spirits with people who weren't heavy drinkers!

Finally, the better you feel about yourself, the less you'll feel you have to prove yourself to your drinking buddies. Strong self-esteem and self-confidence are the antidotes to peer pressure to drink. So the next time you feel the heat to drink, remind yourself of how great you are and how you don't need liquor to feel good about yourself or to make or maintain meaningful friendships.

If you think peer pressure has led to your problem drinking . . .

Identify people who encourage your drinking

Identify your reasons for caving into peer pressure

Minimize the importance of other people's opinions of you

Rethink your relationships with people who want you to drink

Cut ties with people who want you to drink

Limit your time with people who want you to drink

Encourage fellow drinkers to get with the moderate drinking program

Suggest wholesome activities to drinking pals

Cultivate alcohol-free friendships

Cultivate alcohol-free interests

Nurture strong self-esteem to combat peer pressure

You don't need alcohol to feel good about yourself or to make or maintain true relationships

Life Transitions

If you've had a big change in your life and you're drinking to deal with it, alcohol is not the answer. Marriage, divorce, birth, death, kids leaving home, unemployment, financial setbacks, retirement, poor health. Life has it's ups and downs - some good and some bad. But if you rely on booze to see you through these transitions, you might be dealing with addiction too.

Acknowledging shifts and accepting them as a normal part of life is a good start to handling them. Change may not be pleasant sometimes, but it is what it is. And trying to deny it or ignore it might just add to the problem. So be honest with yourself, get your trials and tribulations out in the open and you'll be closer to accepting them and moving on with your life.

When confronting major upsets, allow yourself to experience the full range of emotions that might accompany them. Both positive and negative. Processing the thoughts and feelings that come with upheaval will help you to work through it, instead of prolonging it in an alcoholic haze.

Talking about serious topics with friends might also be helpful. When you talk about a change with thoughtful, trusted friends, you may see the situation more clearly. Before you verbalize your concerns, you might not be able to see the forest for the trees. But once you get them off your chest, you could have greater insight into them and how to deal with them. A friend who is a good listener might be all you need to survive hard times. Joining a support group whose focus is the same as yours may also be healing. Everyone needs a good listener and help at times. And this may be your time to ask for assistance.

Or consider getting professional help - a mental health practitioner, a grief counselor, your clergyman, an employment counselor, your physician, a financial planner, a lawyer. A professional who specializes in the area you're taking on might be beneficial. It will take some weight off your shoulders, so you'll be less inclined to cope with wine. The more help and support you get during a crisis, the better.

Finally, take your time. Take one day at a time. And continue to move forward. You will get through tough transitions in one piece by being kind to yourself, being supported by others and being guided by professionals. There is light and moderate drinking at the end of the tunnel!

If you think a life transition has led to your problem drinking . . .

Acknowledge the change in your life

Accept change as a normal part of life

Allow yourself to feel all of the emotions that come with change

Talk to a trusted friend about transitions in your life

Ask for help

Join a support group

Consider counseling with a mental health professional

Consult professionals knowledgeable about the issues you're facing

Take your time

Take one day at a time

Be kind to yourself during the process

Filling the Void

If something's missing in your life - you're not in a relationship, you've lost your job, your kids have left home, you've moved away from family and friends, you've divorced, you've been widowed or you've retired - and you're using liquor to fill the void, think again. Alcohol won't fill your emptiness. But these simple suggestions will.

Improve your mood without even leaving your neighborhood. Start by making your house a home and get into the domestic arts - get cooking or sewing or cleaning or gardening or crafting. A clean, aromatic house is so comforting. Think about getting a pet. Loving a furry friend makes you feel so good. And it's a fact they can lower your blood pressure and stress levels. Decorate your house with objects and colors that are meaningful to you and evoke good memories. Fixing up your home with things that remind you of good times is fun. Get to know your neighbors a little too. You don't have to be bosom buddies, but connecting with folks close by would give you a sense of belonging. Entertain and have friends over who you like and trust. Breaking bread with good people is therapeutic - and will make you feel whole. Also, do something near and dear to your heart - like volunteering for your favorite charity. You'll feel good about yourself - and fuller - when you do something positive.

Take the energy you've been wasting on feeling sorry for yourself and drinking and redirect it. Get involved in activities you enjoy - athletic, intellectual, social, spiritual, educational, artistic or charitable. Look into interests that have delighted you in the past or ones you've always wanted to get into but never had the time for. Now you've got the time.

Laugh and have as much fun as possible. Fun fills the emptiness and humor - looking at the silly side of life - might be just what you need to feel complete again.

Get out, socialize and develop healthy new relationships. It's so much more entertaining than sitting home alone and drinking. Mingle and get back in the swing of things. When you're surrounded by lively people, you feel full, not empty.

Each day, make a list of ten things that make you happy and commit to doing at least two of them. They might be something as simple as smiling at a stranger, taking a walk or enjoying a great cup of coffee. You'll be filling the hole inside of you with well-being, not tequila.

And focus on all of the wonderful people, events and accomplishments in your life, instead of dwelling on the rotten ones and the emptiness. Obsessing about awful people, disastrous relationships, missed opportunities and mistakes you've made does nothing but bring you down. Concentrate on and be grateful for what you've got and you'll feel better. In fact, everyday make a list of five things you're grateful for. A hot bath, your garden blooming, a good friend, a cozy bed, bacon? Reflect on things that make you feel whole and you'll soon forget about what's missing in your life.

Above all, stop crying in your beer. As long as you're breathing you're still capable of making a fabulous life for yourself. Go out and fill your void - and you'll drink less!

If a void in your life has led to your problem drinking . . .

Make your house a home

Consider getting a pet

Surround yourself with things that remind you of good times

Get to know your neighbors

Entertain friends

Get involved in interesting and fun activities

Cultivate healthy new relationships

Laugh at yourself and your troubles

List ten things that make you happy and commit to two everyday

Focus on the wonderful people, events and accomplishments of your life

Make a list of five things you're grateful for everyday

Stop feeling sorry for yourself and drinking

Go out and fill your void!

Workplace Stress

If you hate your job, you've been downsized, you're always asked to do more, you're called on to perform unfamiliar tasks, you have an impossible boss, you've been asked to sacrifice salary and benefits or you feel you have to work longer and harder just to stay afloat, workplace stress might be fueling your need to drink. You, like so many other people these days, may feel anxious, uncertain and powerless to change or leave your work situation. And you might be taking refuge in the bottle because of these feelings.

If you think you're helpless and have no control over your circumstances, start at the beginning. Discuss the negative aspects of your job with your immediate supervisor, personnel, your union, a grievance committee or a worker's rights organization. If too much responsibility, too little authority or unfair labor practices are getting to you, speak up in a positive, helpful manner. Clearing up a few workplace problems might make your situation bearable.

Both you and your employer should recognize and stick to your job description too. When you have a specific job description, there's no confusion about what's expected of you and what your responsibilities are - taking the pressure off of you.

If you hate your occupation or you don't think you're good at it, but you stick with it because of the money and benefits, start looking around for something you'd really like. Job stress affects so many aspects of your life, it might be worth your while to get into a new line of work that you'd really enjoy or be good at. Life is too short. Of course, this may take some time so be patient, focus on your goal and sooner or later you could land the job of your dreams.

Your work setting may also factor into job-related stress. Poor lighting, ventilation, temperature control, sanitary facilities, too much noise or too little privacy may make your workplace a nightmare. Lack of organization, too much or too little oversight or coping with one crisis after another may also bring you and your job performance down. Get an employee or labor organization to intervene to improve conditions and if that doesn't work, get the Occupational Safety and Health Administration (OSHA) involved. Working in safe, comfortable surroundings is a must if you're going to stress less.

Is your boss the problem? Try to understand where they're coming from. Maybe they're having a tough time in some other area of their life and they're taking it out on you. Hopefully, it will pass. But if it doesn't, you might have to work on your own behavior to improve things. Instead of countering his or her difficult behavior with your own, stop. Try not to react negatively to their negativity. It will only make matters worse. Make an effort to be as cooperative as possible and maybe your supervisor will return the favor.

Don't confront or antagonize the person managing you either. That might just make matters worse. Diplomatically discuss your concerns with them instead. Keeping your cool, explaining exactly what your issues are and brainstorming ways to fix them might better your relationship and working conditions. Just what you want.

If you're criticized by the boss, try not to take it personally. Look at it as a challenge to enhance your job performance. You and your supervisor are partners and both of you want to provide the best product possible. Knowing how you can upgrade your output with input from your manager is crucial. So don't get personal or reactive. This isn't a power struggle, it's a job. However, if these suggestions to improve the relationship between you and your boss don't work over time, perhaps you need to talk to personnel or a human resources professional who could go over other options with you.

If you're overworked, is it possible to reduce your work load? Cut down on the number of hours or days you work? Work from home one, two or three days a week? Don't assume any additional responsibilities. And delegate as many tasks to others as possible.

During the week, have your family pitch in and do household chores to help you out too. Or, if you can afford it, hire out domestic duties. A little more help at home might take some pressure off of you at work.

Finally, remember that stress is in the eye of the beholder. What you may perceive as being stressful, others wouldn't. And putting the people and situations at work in perspective might relieve some strain. When they become too important to you, they get to you. But when you put them in their place - in the back of your mind - they're less likely to affect you.

Know the workplace stressors that push your buttons and drive you to drink. Then respond to them in positive ways - instead of blowing your stack and getting plastered.

If you think workplace stress has led to your problem drinking . . .

Talk to management or a labor organization about your concerns

Be clear about your job description and what's expected of you

If you hate your job, be patient and look for another one

Talk to your supervisor or OSHA about improving workplace conditions

Try to understand your boss

Try to be nice to your boss

Be diplomatic and keep your cool when discussing problems at work

Be positive and constructive when discussing problems at work

Don't take criticism personally

Try to reduce your workload

Don't assume any additional responsibilities

Delegate work to others

Have your family pitch in at home

Hire help for domestic duties if you can afford it

Change the way you perceive your stressors at work

Minimize your workplace stressors and put them in perspective

Beliefs and Expectations About Alcohol

If your conscious or subconscious beliefs and expectations about liquor increase your desire to drink, get smart. Become aware of them and you'll cut down automatically.

Here are safe, realistic beliefs and expectations about drinking and alcohol that reinforce moderate drinking. Healthy drinking usually involves people, socializing and food. It's appropriate drinking - suited to the occasion. It's light drinking and you never get wasted. One or two cocktails are enough to feel happy and relaxed and you don't need more. In fact, more booze is not better - it will just get you drunk and give you a hangover. Moderate drinking can relieve stress - temporarily. Moderate drinking can offer you a few health benefits. And moderate drinking can increase your self-confidence and self-esteem - temporarily. Alcohol abuse, on the other hand, makes you behave impulsively and recklessly. Alcohol abuse can cause or exacerbate negative feelings and moods. Alcohol abuse can ruin your reputation. Alcohol abuse can destroy your relationships. Alcohol abuse can get you into trouble. Alcohol abuse can make you sick. Alcohol abuse can kill you. In general, drinking too much can lead to serious health, psychological, relationship, social, work-related, legal and financial problems. And anyone who drinks too much can become an alcoholic - whether it runs in their family or not.

Now look at dangerous, unrealistic beliefs and expectations about drinking and alcohol that reinforce problem drinking. Drinking is acceptable anytime, anyplace and for any reason. Drinking just to pass the time and getting loaded are okay and nothing to be concerned about. You need more than one or two drinks to have a really good time. In fact, the more liquor you down, the better. Alcohol is an essential social lubricant. Alcohol is needed to fit in. Alcohol helps you to establish and maintain relationships. Alcohol makes you more popular. Alcohol makes you more attractive and sexier. Alcohol makes you smarter. Drinking alcohol, instead of eating, is understandable. Drinking is harmless. Drinking is a good way to entertain yourself if you're bored. Drinking is a good way to take the edge off of loneliness if you're alone. Alcohol-related health, psychological, relationship, social, work-related, legal and financial problems only happen to other people. If alcoholism doesn't run in your family, you'll never become an alcoholic.

What beliefs and expectations about drinking and alcohol do you subscribe to? This very minute, delete the dangerous, unrealistic ones from your brain and stop acting on them. They'll just cause you problems. Then internalize the safe, realistic ones instead - and moderate drinking will come naturally to you!

If beliefs and expectations about drinking and alcohol have led to your problem drinking . . .

Recognize your realistic beliefs and expectations about alcohol

Recognize your unrealistic beliefs and expectations about alcohol

Delete incorrect assumptions about booze from your brain

Stop acting on dangerous assumptions about drinking and alcohol

Internalize safe assumptions about drinking and alcohol

Other Risk Factors

Your age, marital status, employment status, if you have children and your racial, ethnic and cultural background may all influence your drinking. Generally speaking, women who are in their thirties and forties, who are divorced or unemployed and are childless or have no children living at home are at greater risk for problem drinking. And women who are married and work full-time are less inclined to abuse alcohol.

Women between the ages of twenty-one and thirty-four have the highest rates of heavy drinking. Women under forty drink more than women over forty and women over fifty tend to drink less and heavy drinking drops dramatically. But women in their fifties and sixties who are unemployed and have no children at home are more likely to imbibe than their counterparts who are employed and have children at home.

Problem drinking rates are higher among divorced women and women who have never been married. And women who live with a partner, but have never married, are at an even greater risk of developing a drinking problem. Women who are not married but live with a partner are fifty percent more likely to drink heavily than married women!

Hard drinking women get together with hard drinking men - perhaps because they're accepting of each other's bad drinking habits. A happy relationship or marriage can protect you from alcohol abuse. But an unhappy relationship or marriage can increase your odds of it.

White women are in greater danger of hitting the bottle than Hispanic women. And African-American women are least likely to overdrink, compared to other ethnic and racial groups. Cultural attitudes about women and alcohol can shape a woman's drinking behavior.

Just knowing your risk factors will weaken them. You won't fall for them if you're on to them. But if you do find yourself acting inappropriately around spirits because of your background, take a step back. Pull yourself together and challenge your situation with a little self-talk, a little self-control and a few sensible drinking skills. When you cancel these risk factors out, you'll cancel harmful drinking out too!

If you think other risk factors have led to your problem drinking . . .

Identify and challenge the risk factors that affect your drinking

Apply self-talk, self-control and sensible drinking skills to cancel them out

Stop reacting to your risk factors

How Will You Fix the Issues That Drive You to Drink?

You know the underlying problems that trigger your drinking and now you're armed with solutions to deal with them. Take your time, think through your issues and the solutions to them, then devise a comprehensive plan to neutralize each and every one of them so they no longer lead to heavy drinking.

You don't have to be a slave to problems that drive you to drink. You can resolve them. Some might be easier to fix than others, some might require professional help and some you might have to learn to live with. But when you resolve, weaken or accept these alcohol-triggering factors, the easier it will be for you to cut down and acquire a take it or leave it attitude about drinking and alcohol.

First, list all of the issues that influence your drinking. Then, under each one, record all of the healthy ways you can handle it - instead of pouring yourself a stiff one. Decide on the best solution and follow through with it - perhaps the most important step of all. And if your first plan doesn't work, go on to the next until you hit on one that does.

Hang in there! Many of these problems didn't happen overnight and they won't be resolved overnight. But perseverance will payoff in most cases. And with a good plan, patience and time you will prevail.

When you fix the deeper issues that spark your alcohol appetite, you'll not only drink less, you'll improve the quality of your life too!

Fix the issues behind your problem drinking . . .

List the underlying issues that influence your drinking

Brainstorm and record healthy solutions to these issues

Follow through with your plans

Be patient

Watch your alcohol consumption do down automatically

Enjoy a better quality of life

Step Five

Keep Up the Good Work!

∽ *Chapter 10* ∽

Enjoy Your Moderate Drinking Mindset and Lifestyle Forever!

Y ou've built your healthy drinking mentality and way of life from the ground up, now reinforce them so you don't fall back into bad habits. You haven't gone to all this trouble just to revert back to your old problem drinking patterns! And here are thirteen powerful pointers enabling you to own your enriched lifestyle forever.

1. Learn to Be Happy Without Liquor!

If you can have fun and be happy without alcohol, you'd have it made and wouldn't need a moderate drinking program. Booze wouldn't take center stage in your life. You'd drink responsibly without giving it a second thought. And you'd never get drunk. You'd always drink safely and appropriately and enjoy a take it or leave it attitude about spirits.

Being proactive and going out of your way to develop relationships and hobbies that don't involve liquor is one fool-proof way you can be happy without wine. Yes, it may take some time and energy to cultivate new alcohol-free friendships and interests. But it would be worth it in the long run. You wouldn't rely on vodka to feel good, it would become less important to you and you'd drink less instinctively. Payoffs!

So the next time you're thinking about drinking, think about connecting with people and getting involved in entertainment that doesn't focus on alcohol instead. You'll learn to be happy without liquor!

2. Practice the Drink/Link Format Every Week

The Drink/Link Format is a two-part exercise where you examine your drinking behavior for the previous week and preplan it for the coming week. If you faithfully check in with yourself once a week with the format, it will be easier for you to stay within your limits and you'll succeed at moderate drinking permanently.

First, look at the past week and ask yourself these questions. How many drinks did I have? Did I ever go over my daily drink limit? Did I go over my weekly drink limit? Did I ever deviate from my drinking plans? What factors triggered my drinking? If I over drank, what factors triggered my overdrinking? What were my greatest challenges within the last week?

If you went over your daily or weekly drink limits, you deviated from your drinking plans or you noticed certain triggers that led to heavier drinking, heads up. It's up to you to figure out what went wrong so you can stick to your limits in the future. If specific triggers got the best of you, devise a concrete plan to defuse them. All that's left for you to do is to put your plan into action so when the time comes you can avoid another problem drinking outcome.

Now look at your coming week. Schedule a couple of alcohol-free days right off the bat. Days you're so busy there's no time for drinking or relaxing days when nothing's going on are good days to abstain. Next, look at all of the potential drinking situations that might come up during the week. Social engagements, game night, a book club get-together, drinking at home? It's your responsibility to make a drinking plan for each and every one of these occasions. How many drinks will you have? How long will you drink? What moderate drinking tools and concepts will you use to stay within your limits? What will be your greatest challenges? How will you handle them? Leave nothing to chance and you'll increase the odds of you sticking to your drink limits. And re-member - plans are just meaningless words unless you actually apply them.

Practice the format week in and week out and you'll feel more and more comfortable with your healthy new drinking habits. And eventual-ly, you'll no longer have to count drinks or even make plans. You'll enjoy light, problem-free drinking effortlessly!

3. Continue to Monitor Your Drinking

Keeping tabs on your drinking even after you've completed the program is crucial for your long-term success. Everyday or every time you drink, record the number of drinks you have or, better yet, continue to keep your drinking diary. Counting your drinks keeps you on your toes. You won't become complacent or engage in mindless drinking if you continue to tally your cocktails.

Record your alcohol consumption or keep your diary for at least three months after you've finished the program. Or longer, if you think it will prevent you from going astray. It's a worthwhile exercise that will keep you on the straight and narrow.

4. Listen to the Moderate Drinking Voice Inside of Your Head

Believe it or not, there's a little voice inside of your head that tells you when it's time to slow down or stop drinking. You may not even be aware of it, but it's there and it's waiting for you to listen to it. Most often, it speaks to you when you're under a .06 BAC. And it tells you to pace yourself or quit drinking.

Pay attention to that moderate drinking voice inside of your head! Instead of turning a deaf ear to it and drinking like there's no tomorrow, listen to it and act on it. Next time you drink, can you hear it?

5. Small Steps Add Up to Big Changes

Changing your ways doesn't happen overnight. Rome wasn't built in a day. And it doesn't happen in large increments. No, changing your drinking ways happens with small steps over time. And gradually, the sum of these small steps will add up to a big improvement in your drinking habits and reduced alcohol consumption. That's how change happens!

So start with little adjustments at first. They may seem insignificant, but eventually they'll get the moderate drinking job done.

6. You Don't Break Bad Habits, You Replace Them

You don't suddenly break bad drinking habits. No, you gradually replace them with healthy new ones. That's another way change happens. So get that old notion of "breaking" bad habits out of your head and "replacing" them into it.

When you're tempted to revert back to your old problem drinking patterns, substitute healthy new ones for them instead. You'll be making a positive transition if you do.

7. Cultivate Greater Self-Control Around Alcohol

You can assert greater self-control over your drinking. It is possible to get better at managing booze. The secret is to start simple.

Begin with easy things, like delaying for ten minutes between drinks or alternating with a soft drink. When you succeed at these small improvements, you'll not only increase your self-control around alcohol, you'll increase your self-confidence too - and you'll feel more capable of conquering bigger challenges ahead. And eventually, you'll feel in charge of spirits, not the other way around.

8. Meaningful Change Requires a Little Sacrifice

No pain, no gain. Change always involves a little sacrifice. At times, you're going to have to say no to impulses that have become bad habits. And it might feel a little awkward and uncomfortable at first.

But you will be rewarded for going outside of your comfort zone and saying no to unhealthy impulses. It will get easier. And you'll become a safe, moderate drinker with a take it or leave attitude about alcohol. Payoff!

Remember - a change for the better might not always feel good - especially in the beginning. But think of your life long-term - no more liquor problems - ever. Hang tough!

9. Don't Always Equate Alcohol with a Good Time

If you think a cocktail always makes for a good time, think again. Sure, sometimes when you're mildly high you enjoy yourself. But there are lots of bad things that happen when you drink too. Especially if you drink too much. Arguments, blackouts, accidents, dangerous situations. You can hurt or kill yourself or someone else when you're loaded. In fact, booze can lead to some pretty awful predicaments if you're not careful.

You probably have a selective memory when it comes to alcohol and good times. Just remind yourself that being under the influence doesn't always end well. That sobering thought might just keep you in control and out of trouble.

10. Challenge Dangerous Drinking Moods

Say you're having a terrible day, you're in a rotten mood and you ask yourself who cares if you go over your limit? You don't. Why not just continue drinking?

You're only human so you're bound to have these "why not?" or "who cares?" feelings at times - when staying within your limits is the furthest thing from your mind. And even though these moods are understandable, they're dangerous to the healthy new drinking habits you're establishing. With this kind of thinking you throw the baby out with the bathwater and forget all about your moderate drinking commitment and the program. And you might get wasted.

What can you possibly do or say to yourself when you're feeling defeated and want to drink without any rules? How can you prevent a slip from happening when you're in the dumps? First, get a grip, take a step back and give yourself a stirring motivational pep talk where you review all of your very good reasons for cutting down. Then fantasize about how much better your life will be when you're a social drinker. Maybe that will get you passionate about moderating again. A healthy, happy life is so much more important to you than temporarily seeing pink elephants! So before you give in to the impulse to ditch the program and drink to your heart's content, chill out, get a grip and get back in the game with a pep talk.

Take a time out. Just because you want to toss the program doesn't mean you have to do it immediately. Take a ten minute breather from this intense drinking desire. Relax. You might come to your senses.

Consider a pleasant distracting activity too. You might forget all about how miserable you feel or drinking your troubles away. It would be wise for you to have some fabulous distracting activity already up your sleeve to counter this devil-may-care attitude when it pops up. Don't drink - treat yourself to your favorite food, get a massage, go on a serious shopping spree, take a hike or soak in a bubble bath instead. It might take your mind off of the urge and keep you in line.

Think about and plan for times when you could care less about regulating your drinking. And remind yourself that a great pep talk, taking a time out and swinging into an enjoyable activity are effective ways to beat those "why not?" and "who cares?" blues. If you can master these dangerous drinking moods without giving in to them, there's no doubt you can master your drinking too!

11. Be Patient

Moderate drinking thinking and habits aren't automatic for most problem drinkers. They happen over time if you're faithful to the program. And gradually, you reach your ultimate goals - effortless healthy drinking and a take it or leave it attitude about alcohol.

So be patient with yourself and your brand new thinking and behavior. You're in this for the long haul and it will take some time for you to acquire a moderate drinking mindset and lifestyle. For some, it may only take three or four months. For others, it may take a year. And some individuals might have to practice the program for two or three years to settle into worry-free, responsible drinking forever. Stick to the program - through good times and bad - and change will happen.

12. Identify Obstacles to Your Safe New Drinking Behavior

Being aware of and keeping an eye on factors that might sabotage your new drinking habits would be worth your while. If you know what your downfalls are, you can deal with them before they become problematic.

What internal or external drinking triggers do you struggle with? What unresolved, underlying problems in your life continue to fuel your alcohol appetite? Identify them, understand the negative impact they have on you and neutralize them so they no longer enter into your drinking equation. List any obstacles that may come between you and moderate drinking.

Just acknowledging them might put them to rest. Or addressing them and resolving them will. Perhaps looking at them in a different light will cancel them out. Or accepting them and moving on with your life will.

Recognizing and dealing with stumbling blocks to your sensible drinking behavior is a must - if you're going to enjoy safe, social drinking for the rest of your life.

13. Don't Settle

At certain times in your life you've probably dealt with difficult people or situations with a cocktail in your hand. You've felt powerless, so you empowered yourself with a vodka tonic. Or you've waited for change to happen - with a stiff one. Hopefully, this passive attitude and lifestyle which has encouraged and supported your problem drinking is a thing of the past.

Here, you've learned to be proactive and tackle problems that have impacted your life and your drinking. You've learned, instead of feeling helpless and hopeless and guzzling, to take charge and fix issues that make you unhappy and drive you to drink. You don't have to be miserable biding your time, wishing for a better life and drinking your problems away. You have the power to change! To design a wonderful life for yourself! And when you feel your power and put it to work for you, moderate drinking will follow.

Settling for an imperfect life and thinking you can't do anything about it is the recipe for alcohol abuse. Not settling for an imperfect life and taking on your problems is the recipe for sensible drinking.

Enjoy Your Moderate Drinking Mindset and Lifestyle Forever!

1. Learn to be Happy Without Liquor!
2. Practice the Drink/Link Format Every Week
3. Continue to Monitor Your Drinking
4. Listen to the Moderate Drinking Voice Inside of Your Head
5. Small Steps Add Up to Big Changes
6. You Don't Break Bad Habits, You Replace Them
7. Cultivate Greater Self-Control Around Alcohol
8. Meaningful Change Requires a Little Sacrifice
9. Don't Always Equate Alcohol with a Good Time
10. Challenge Dangerous Drinking Moods
11. Be Patient
12. Identify Obstacles to Your Moderate Drinking Behavior
13. Don't Settle

∞ *Chapter 11* ∞

What If You Slip?

I t's only natural to think about reverting back to your old drinking habits at times. In fact, a slip is a normal part of the change process for most of us. So learning from your lapse, instead of letting it get the best of you, is your goal. If you can make a positive experience out of a negative one - like knowing what led to the slip and how to avoid it in the future - you'll be well on your way to improved drinking habits and reduced alcohol consumption forever.

In case you slip, here are nine great tips on how to handle it so it doesn't defeat you. Don't wallow in self-pity if you blow it. Get smart about it and get back on the program!

A Slip or a Relapse?

A slip is a single, isolated incident where you deviate from your healthy new drinking habits and overindulge. But a relapse is when you revert back to problem drinking for a week or more.

Whether it's a major blip or a minor one, you need to pick yourself up, dust yourself off, analyze what went wrong and how you can prevent it from happening in the future - so you can move forward with your wholesome new way of life.

Acknowledge the Slip

If you don't acknowledge a slip or a relapse happened, you'll never be able to learn from it and get over it. So be honest with yourself and look it straight in the eye. Admitting you made a mistake is the first step to fixing it.

Process Negative Feelings

When you've taken a step back, feeling bad about yourself is par for the course. You feel ashamed and guilty and your self-esteem and self-confidence take a beating. You feel like a failure. And getting back on the program is probably the last thing on your mind.

Allow yourself to process these feelings. Reflect on them. Then get them out of your system. Those awful feelings you're having about yourself are counterproductive - they erode your self-esteem and self-confidence even further and make it even harder for you to get back on track. And if you continue to dwell on them, you'll remain in your old heavy drinking pattern.

So get into your feelings, then write them off - because the longer you brood about what a terrible person you are, the harder it will be for you to resume the program.

Learn From Your Slip

You need to play detective if you're going to turn a mistake into a positive learning experience. Start by retracing your steps and examining all of the variables that might have led to your overdrinking episode. Were external cues - people, places or circumstances - to blame? Were internal cues - hunger, fatigue, moods or emotions - the culprits? Was a combination of internal and external cues behind your problem drinking meltdown? Were nagging, underlying issues responsible for your blip? Or was the perfect storm of drinking triggers and deeper issues the villain? Identifying the variables that led you astray is critical if you want to get smart about your setback.

Once you've put your finger on the cues that led to your downfall, think about how you'll tweak them so they'll no longer trip your old drinking habits. Look at each cue individually and either treat it appropriately, eliminate it, limit your exposure to it, weaken it or change the way you think about it - so it no longer tempts you into going all out. Examine the profound issues that drive you to drink too. Are your plans to put them to rest working? Then look at the big picture and understand why, when all of these triggers and issues converged, you caved in and drank too much.

Finally, devise a comprehensive plan to defuse these cues and concerns the next time you're caught up in them. Preplan exactly what you'll do and say to yourself when you're faced with the same set of risky circumstances. The only thing left for you to do is to follow through with your plan! Nothing will be left to chance the next time you're thinking about letting loose, so you'll be less likely to let loose.

Analyzing your errors and preplanning how you'll manage them in the future may be all you need to enjoy light drinking long-term. Do it!

Resolve to Do Better in the Future

Now that you know how to constructively deal with a slip and learn from it, you have to resolve to do better the next time you're challenged. You've got lots of moderate drinking skills and strategies under your belt, so all you have to do is to make up your mind to behave differently when hazardous conditions pop up again.

This very minute, vow to follow through with your slip fix - your plan to defuse dangerous drinking triggers and issues - so when you're faced with the same hazardous conditions you won't fall back again. You can succeed at moderate drinking - if you resolve to do better the next time around.

Now Get Back on Track

Restart the program immediately after you've admitted your slip, processed your feelings, learned what went wrong, devised plans to cancel out risky drinking cues and issues and resolved to do better in the future.

It's time for you to move forward and stop wasting your precious energy thinking badly about yourself and the mistakes you've made. Pick up the pieces and get back on the behavior change track right now. It's a new day!

A Slip Might Deter You

Even though you shouldn't be crushed by a slip, it wouldn't be a bad idea for you to remind yourself of it occasionally. Remember the physical and psychological hangovers you had the day after you fell off of the moderate drinking wagon? How long did it take you to recover? Did you engage in ugly or unsafe behavior when you were loaded? How long did it take for you to undo the damage you did to yourself or others when you blew it? If you remind yourself of what a mess you were when you exceeded your limit, compared to how great you feel when you drink sensibly, reminiscing about a slip might be a valuable tool for you.

So the next time you're tempted to ignore the program, just think about how awful you felt when you fell off of it. That thought might deter you from engaging in the same reckless behavior in the future!

Review the Drink/Link Change Your Drinking Behavior Formula

You should be feeling better by now. You've got the skills to learn from your setback and return to your healthy new habits. Now take a minute for a little refresher course on the Drink/Link Change Your Drinking Behavior Formula. You need to re-examine it and figure out which element or elements of this formula you should brush up on so you'll never slip again.

You do remember the Drink/Link Change Your Drinking Behavior Formula: one part motivation that generates the energy you need to change your ways, one part moderate drinking tools and concepts that provide the means for you to stay within your drink limits and one part positive reinforcement that rewards you for your successes and deeply ingrains your safe new drinking habits.

If you've slipped or relapsed, one of these components probably wasn't in play. So take your time and think about the parts of this formula that are your weak points. Not stoking your motivation? Not applying the moderate drinking skills to your behavior? Not rewarding yourself for a job well done?

When you figure out what your weak points are and you strengthen them, the less likely you'll have problems down the road. A gentle reminder . . .

Recommit Yourself to Moderate Drinking

At the beginning of the program you were asked to make a firm commitment to moderate drinking. Remember? You should have written down your commitment - and all of your reasons for wanting to drink less - so you could refer to them at any time. Especially when you were wavering.

Think back to why you wanted to clean up your drinking act in the first place. Think about all the benefits you'll reap when you lower your alcohol consumption. Daydream about how much better you'll feel and the healthier relationships you'll enjoy. Fantasize about having more energy and fun and feeling good about yourself. Envision how fabulous your life will be - without so much liquor. And how you'll never worry about alcohol-related health, psychological, social, work, financial or legal problems again.

Recommit yourself to moderate drinking right now and don't look back. You've learned from your slip and you're past it. Now focus on the wonderful life ahead of you - if you remain committed to the program and responsible drinking.

What If You Slip?

Is it a slip or a relapse?

Acknowledge the slip

Process negative feelings

Learn from your slip

Resolve to do better in the future

Get back on track no matter what

A slip might deter you

Review the Drink/Link Change Your Drinking Behavior Formula

Recommit yourself to moderate drinking

∞ Chapter 12 ∞

Keep Your Mind and Other Options Open

I s sticking to the program difficult for you? Do you go over your drink limit often? Do you slip or relapse often? Is it hard for you to get back on track? You may need a more intensive moderation approach that includes personal counseling. The guidance and support you'd get from a trained professional might increase your chances of success.

Or is trying to control your drinking more trouble than it's worth? Do you think stopping altogether would be easier? Abstinence might be the best option for you. Being straight with yourself and recognizing that moderate drinking just isn't working takes courage. But you've got it and you're taking good care of yourself when you acknowledge abstinence as the most effective solution to your drinking problem.

Whether you decide to stick with moderate drinking or quit altogether, here are some resources that might be helpful to you.

Al-Anon Family Group/Alateen

www.al-anon.alateen.org

Al-Anon Family Group/Alateen is a fellowship for relatives and friends of people with alcohol problems. Alateen is primarily for teenagers. The philosophy behind it is adapted from Alcoholics Anonymous and the Twelve Step Program.

Alcoholics Anonymous

www.aa.org

1-212-870-3400

AA is an international fellowship of men and women who have alcohol problems. Membership is open to anyone who wants to do something about their drinking. AA offers a philosophy and plan to live a satisfying life without alcohol and members share their experiences at meetings. All-women meetings are available in some areas.

For more information about AA or to find meetings, call them, go to their website or check your phone book for local listings.

Drink/Link Moderate Drinking Programs

www.drinklinkmoderation.com

Email: info@drinklinkmoderation.com

Toll-Free: 1-888-773-7465

Established in 1988 by Donna Cornett, Drink/Link was the first moderate drinking program in the United States registered with both the United States Department of Health and Human Services and the California Department of Alcohol and Drug Programs.

Drink/Link is a seven-week program that offers safe-drinking guidelines and clinically-proven behavioral, cognitive, motivational and lifestyle strategies and techniques to help you stay within moderate drinking limits. Drink/Link offers a confidential Telephone Counseling Program, an Email Counseling Program and a Self-Study Program.

Moderate Drinking My Way Program

www.moderatedrinkingmyway.com

Email: info@drinklinkmoderation.com

Toll-Free: 1-888-773-7465

The Moderate Drinking My Way Program, developed by Donna Cornett in 2012, is designed specifically for women and is an offshoot of the Drink/Link Moderate Drinking Program.

It's a female-friendly, drug-free five-step program based on safe-drinking concepts and guidelines and it offers clinically-proven behavioral, cognitive, motivational and lifestyle skills and strategies empowering you to reduce your alcohol craving and consumption, prevent alcoholism and resolve women-specific issues that drive you to drink. It's more than a drinking program, it's a lifestyle program that encourages you to cultivate a moderate drinking mindset and lifestyle so you drink less naturally and get the most out of life.

The Moderate Drinking My Way Program Telephone Counseling Program and Email Counseling Program offer confidential conversations with Donna Cornett personally.

National Association for Children of Alcoholics

www.nacoa.net

An organization that works on behalf of children of alcohol and drug dependent parents.

National Clearinghouse for Alcohol and Drug Information

www.ncadi.samhsa.gov

Provides alcohol and drug abuse information produced by the Substance Abuse Mental Health Services Administration, U.S. Department of Health and Human Services.

National Council on Alcoholism and Drug Dependence

www.ncadd.org

Provides telephone numbers of local NCADD affiliates who provide information on local treatment resources and educational materials on alcoholism.

National Drug and Alcohol Treatment Referral Routing Service

www.niaaa,nih.gov/faq/faqhtm.

Toll-Free: 1-800-662-HELP

Speak to someone about an alcohol problem and get more information about treatment programs in your local community.

National Institute on Alcohol Abuse and Alcoholism

www.niaaa.nih.gov

The NIAAA offers information on a wide variety of topics, including fetal alcohol syndrome, the dangers of mixing alcohol with medications, family history of alcoholism, and preventing underage drinking. It also offers a free 12-minute video, A Woman's Health Issue, profiling women recovering from alcohol problems and describing the health consequences of heavy drinking in women.

National Institute on Alcohol Abuse and Alcoholism Substance Abuse Treatment Facility Locator

www.findtreatment.samhsa.gov

Provides alcohol and drug abuse information and treatment referral assistance produced by the Substance Abuse Mental Health Services Administration, U.S. Department of Health and Human Services.

Women for Sobriety

www.womenforsobriety.org

Email: newlife@nni.com

1-215-536-8026

Established in 1976 by Jean Kirkpatrick, the Women for Sobriety New Life Program was the first self-help abstinence program designed specifically for women. It's for any woman wanting to overcome alcoholism or any other addiction and it takes into account the special problems women have in recovery. It's based on thirteen acceptance statements which empower women to change their thinking and actions about their life, emotions and alcohol. It offers literature and has support groups in some areas.

What Works for You?

If these options are helpful to you, great! You've got even more re-sources to see you through to your moderation or abstinence goal. But if they aren't, get busy and go online, go to the library or contact your local health department for agencies and programs that will be.

Don't be shy about asking for help. We all need a little support at times. Besides, you'll come to terms with your drinking problem sooner rather than later if you get the assistance you need early on.

Take the initiative. Then get on with your wonderful life!

About
Donna J. Cornett, M.A.

Donna J. Cornett is the founder and director of Drink/Link Moderate Drinking Programs and the Moderate Drinking My Way Program. She holds an M.A. and California College Teaching Credential in psychology and believes offering drinkers a moderate drinking goal, instead of life-long abstinence, is the key to motivating them to seek early treatment and preventing alcohol abuse.

Cornett was in her thirties when she realized she was drinking too much and would be facing a serious drinking problem if she didn't address it. At that time, her only options were abstinence, AA or to keep on drinking. There was no middle-of-the-road alcohol education program teaching drinkers sensible drinking habits and attitudes so they could avoid problem drinking. And like so many other drinkers, she did not believe her drinking was serious enough to stop altogether or in the concept of a higher power to cut down.

Consequently, Cornett developed Drink/Link in 1988 - long before any other moderate drinking program was available in the United States. This commonsense program teaches you to modify your drinking habits, reduce your alcohol craving and consumption and prevent alcoholism. In 2012, she developed the Moderate Drinking My Way Program just for women - empowering you to drink less, improve your drinking habits, resolve women-specific issues that drive you to drink and cultivate a moderate drinking mindset and lifestyle so you drink less naturally and get the most out of life.

Donna J. Cornett is also the author of *7 Weeks to Safe Social Drinking*, *Moderate Drinking - Naturally!*, *The Moderate Drinking Made Easy Workbook* and *Beat Binge Drinking*. She is an expert in the field of behavior change and has been featured or consulted for articles in Time Magazine, the New York Post, ABCNews.com, WebMD.com, Esquire,

169

Scripps Howard News Service and other professional publications. Cornett lives in the wine country in Northern California.

Drink/Link Moderate Drinking Programs SM
P.O. Box 5441
Santa Rosa, California, USA 95402
www.drinklinkmoderation.com
Email: donna@drinklinkmoderation.com
Toll-Free: 1-888-773-7465
Local: 1-707-539-5465

About the Moderate Drinking℠ My Way Program

The Moderate Drinking My Way Program is designed specifically for women and is an offshoot of the Drink/Link Moderate Drinking Program. It's based on commonsense, safe-drinking guidelines and offers you clinically-proven behavioral, cognitive, motivational and lifestyle strategies and techniques empowering you to reduce your alcohol craving and consumption, prevent alcoholism and resolve women-specific issues that drive you to drink. It's more than just a drinking program, it's a lifestyle program that encourages you to cultivate a moderate drinking mindset and way of life so you drink less naturally and get the most out of life.

Donna Cornett personally offers confidential counseling with the Moderate Drinking My Way Telephone Counseling Program and the Email Counseling Program. Feel free to email or call her if you have any questions or concerns about the program or your drinking.

The Moderate Drinking My Way Program ℠
P.O. Box 5441
Santa Rosa, California, USA 95402
www.moderatedrinkingmyway.com
Email: donna@drinklinkmoderation.com
Toll-Free: 1-888-773-7465
Local: 1-707-539-5465

About
Donna J. Cornett's Books

Donna Cornett has written four other books. *7 Weeks to Safe Social Drinking: How to Effectively Moderate Your Alcohol Intake* offers a comprehensive self-help moderate drinking program to reduce your alcohol craving and consumption, improve your drinking habits, prevent alcoholism and make liquor less important in your life.

Moderate Drinking - Naturally! Herbs and Vitamins to Control Your Drinking explores ancient alternative medicine remedies - nutritional and herbal supplements and Chinese, Ayurvedic and Homeopathic alcohol abuse treatments - to reduce your drinking desire so you drink less naturally.

The *Moderate Drinking Made Easy Workbook: Drinker-Friendly Tips and Exercises to Control Drinking and Reduce Alcohol Craving and Consumption* is a unique workbook that gives you simple before drinking, during drinking and after drinking tips and exercises to help you stay within moderate drinking limits.

Beat Binge Drinking: A Smart Drinking Guide for Teens, College Students and Young Adults Who Choose to Drink is the first and only complete guide to alcohol use designed specifically for young adults - empowering them with responsible drinking guidelines and tips to reduce their alcohol consumption and prevent binge drinking.

All of these books are available on amazon.com, barnesandnoble.com, at major book retailers and at Drink/Link Moderate Drinking Programs and Products at www.drinklinkmoderation.com.

Bibliography

Alcoholics Anonymous World Services, Inc. Information on Alcoholics Anonymous. New York: 2011. www.aa.org.

American Psychological Association. Anxiety disorders and effective treatment. Psychology Help Center, 2010. www.apa.org.

American Psychological Association. Attention deficit hyperactivity disorder. Psychology Topics, 2000. www.apa.org.

American Psychological Association. Bipolar disorder. Psychology Topics, 2000. www.apa.org.

American Psychological Association. Managing your boss. Psychology Help Center, 2012. www.apa.org.

American Psychological Association. Obsessive-compulsive disorder. Psychology Topics, 2000. www.apa.org.

American Psychological Association. Post-traumatic stress disorder. Psychology Topics, 2000. www.apa.org.

American Psychological Association. Strategies for controlling your anger. Spielberger, C. and Deffenbacher, J., Psychology Help Center, 2011. www.apa.org.

American Psychological Association. Stress tip sheet. Psychology Help Center, 2012. www.apa.org.

American Psychological Association. Understanding depression and effective treatment. Abrahamson, D., Homyak. L and Rehm, L., Psychology Help Center, 2010. www.apa.org.

Bepko, C., ed. *Feminism and Addiction.* New York: Haworth Press, 1991.

Bepko, C. and Krestan, J. *Too Good for Her Own Good: Searching for Self and Intimacy in Important Relationships.* New York: HarperPerennial, 1990.

Chida, Y. and Steptoe, A. "The association of anger and hostility with future coronary heart disease: A metanalytic review of prospective evidence." *Journal of the American College of Cardiology* 53(11): 936-946, 2009.

Cornett, D. *7 Weeks to Safe Social Drinking: How to Effectively Moderate Your Alcohol Intake.* Santa Rosa, California: People Friendly Books, 2011.

Cornett, D. *Beat Binge Drinking: A Smart Drinking Guide for Teens, College Students and Young Adults Who Choose to Drink.* Santa Rosa, California: People Friendly Books, 2010.

Cornett, D. *Moderate Drinking Naturally: Herbs and Vitamins to Control Your Drinking.* Santa Rosa, California: People Friendly Books, 2005.

Cornett, D. *The Moderate Drinking Made Easy Workbook: Drinker-Friendly Tips and Exercises to Control Drinking and Reduce Alcohol Craving and Consumption.* Santa Rosa, California: People Friendly Books, 2009.

Deffenbacher, J.L. "Angry drivers: characteristics and clinical interventions." *Revista Mexicana de Psicologia* 26(1): 5-16, 2009.

Fuchs, C.S., Stampfer, M.J. and Colditz, G.A., et al. "Alcohol consumption and mortality among women." Harvard Nurses Health Study. *New England Journal of Medicine* 332 (19): 1245-1250, 1995.

Jersild, D. *Happy Hours.* New York: HarperCollins Publishers Inc, 2000.

Jewell, R. *My Way Out.* Anchorage, Alaska: Capalo Press, 2005.

Jones, P. "The female partner of the recovering male alcoholic: a comparative review of three methods of family therapy, including a feminist perspective." *Behavioral Medicine Associates*, 2012. www.bma-wellness.com.

Kazdin, A.E., ed. *Encyclopedia of Psychology.* New York: Oxford University Press USA, 2000.

McCloskey, M.S. and Noblett, K.L., et al. "Cognitive-behavioral therapy for intermittent explosive disorder: a pilot randomized clinical trial." *Journal of Consulting and Clinical Psychology* 79(5): 876-876, 2008.

Miller, L. *The Stress Solution.* New York: Random House Value Publishing, 1995.

National Institute on Alcohol Abuse and Alcoholism Publications. "Alcohol: a woman's health issue. " *Alcohol Alert* No. 62, 2004.

National Institute on Alcohol Abuse and Alcoholism Publications. "Are women more vulnerable to alcohol's effects?" *Alcohol Alert* No. 46, 1999.

National Institute on Alcohol Abuse and Alcoholism Publications. Women and Alcohol, 2011. http://pubs.niaaa.nih.gov.

Nolen-Hoeksema, S. *Eating, Drinking, Overthinking: The Toxic Triangle of Food, Alcohol, and Depression - and How Women Can Break Free.* New York: Henry Holt Company, 2006.

The National Center on Addiction and Substance Abuse at Columbia University. *Women Under the Influence.* Baltimore, MD: Johns Hopkins University Press, 2006.

United States Departments of Agriculture and Health and Human Services. *U.S. Dietary Guidelines for Americans, 2010.* www.dietaryguidelines.gov.

University of Colorado Department of Alcohol and Drug Prevention and Education. "Numeric Blood Alcohol Level Chart." University of Colorado.

Vimont, C. "Gender differences emerge in alcohol use disorder treatment." July, 2011. www.drugfree.org.

Wilsnack, S.C. and Wilsnack, R.L., eds. *Gender and Alcohol: Individual and Social Perspectives.* New Brunswick, N.J.: Rutgers Center of Alcohol Studies, 1997.

Women for Sobriety, Inc. *The Collection of Sobering Thoughts Booklet, Volume 1.* Quakertown, PA, 1976-1977.

Made in the USA
Las Vegas, NV
18 September 2021